Dear Ruby Ann

Other books by
Ruby Ann Boxcar

Ruby Ann's Down Home Trailer Park Cookbook
Ruby Ann's Down Home Trailer Park Holiday Cookbook
Ruby Ann's Down Home Trailer Park BBQin' Cookbook
Ruby Ann's Down Home Trailer Park Guide to Livin' Real Good

Donna Sue's Down Home Trailer Park Bartending Guide
(Foreword by Ruby Ann Boxcar)

Dear Ruby Ann

Down Home Advice About Lovin', Livin', and

the Whole Shebang

RUBY ANN BOXCAR

CITADEL PRESS
Kensington Publishing Corp.
www.kensingtonbooks.com

CITADEL PRESS books are published by

Kensington Publishing Corp.
850 Third Avenue
New York, NY 10022

All Kensington titles, imprints, and distributed lines are available at special quantity discounts for bulk purchases for sales promotions, premiums, fund-raising, educational, or institutional use. Special book excerpts or customized printings can also be created to fit specific needs. For details, write or phone the office of the Kensington special sales manager: Kensington Publishing Corp., 850 Third Avenue, New York, NY 10022, attn: Special Sales Department, phone 1-800-221-2647.

Photos by Ruby Ann's husband, Dew

The following are trademarks of their respective owners, who do not endorse this book: Amway, Aqua Net, Ben-Gay, Botox, Buster Bar, Butterfinger, Comet, Cool Whip, Count Chocula, Crisco, Crock-Pot, Dairy Queen, Day-Timer, diet Coke, Ding Dongs, Dr Pepper, eBay, Eveready, Ex-Lax, Fingerhut, Frontline, Fruit Loops, Glad, Gold Bond, Golden Corral, Goldfish crackers, Hartz, Ho Hos, Huggies, Jean Naté, Jell-O, Kmart, Lava, La-Z-Boy, Lucky Strike, Lycra, Maytag, Miracle Whip, Monopoly, Mountain Dew, Naturalizers, Nyquil, Old Milwaukee, Oxyclean, Parkay, Piggly Wiggly, Plexiglas, Pontiac, Prozac, RC Cola, Red Lobster, Rice-A-Roni, Ritz, Schlitz, Scotch tape, Shout, Skin-so-soft, Spam, Stetson, Tastee-Freez, Tickle Me Elmo doll, TiVo, Tracker, Tupperware, Turtle Wax, Twinkies, Velveeta, Wal-Mart, Welch's, and Wesson oil.

This book is for entertainment purposes. Advice and recommendations contained in this book should be read with the humorous spirit in which they are intended.

First printing: May 2004

10 9 8 7 6 5 4 3 2 1

Printed in the United States of America

Library of Congress Control Number 2004100513

ISBN 0-8065-2560-6

This here book is dedicated to my assistant, Kevin, who's put his dreams of findin' a wife and startin' a family on the back burner just so he can follow me around the world, makin' sure that I look as good as I do for all my deservin' fans when I'm out on the road. Thanks.

Contents

On the road again: Ruby Ann with Kevin.

Preface

*R*egardless of how heavy my load might be, or how long my journey has gone on, I continue ahead without complainin' 'cause I know that folks all around this world are constantly keepin' their eyes on me as a sort of beacon of hope or a goal, if you will, for them to try and emulate. "If Ruby Ann can make it," they say to themselves, "then I know I can make it, too." And even though this world might be a tough row to hoe, and I mean that in a good Baptist way of course, I know that many of y'all out there are able to hoe a little easier 'cause of me. Why look at all the hoein' my older sister, Donna Sue, has done over the years. I can't help but think that, just like y'all, she was able to do it a little easier 'cause of my inspiration and example of turnin' bad things into good. I know that my dear friend Tammy Faye Bakker Messner says, "When life hands you lemons, make lemonade." Well, I've been makin' fertilizer! But I'm not complainin'. And the thing is that y'all know that, which is why you keep me in sight, and why y'all are always lookin' to me for the answers to your problems.

Turnin' to one another in times of heartache has always been the trailer park way. I think that's partly 'cause we're so carin' about other people as well as about our own tiny community. And you'll find this to be true in most every trailer park. We're always happy to have you stop by and tell us your problems over a glass of sweet tea. Of course sometimes some of us are also happy to jump on the phone just as soon as you leave and share your problems with others as well. I've got to admit that I do that, too, but I do it in more of a way of sharin' an example, if you will, with another person who's goin' through the same type of thing that you've been goin' through. And that explains this book that you've either just bought, borrowed from a friend, or have been given as a gift.

As y'all will soon see, I get cards, letters, and e-mails from folks all around the world. Seein' how important each and everyone of y'all is to me, I take the time to read and answer each of these with a bit of advice that I think will help the person solve the quandary he's concerned about. I do this 'cause I know what it's like to hurt inside or to have your life in turmoil, which can be as close to hell as a Baptist can get. As President Clinton said, "I feel your pain." And I do. I understand the utter despair that one can carry around with 'em because of a crisis that they're facin', which is another reason I take the time to help you find the answer. Of course I delete the e-mails that are in a foreign language and take the cards and letters that ain't in English and throw those in the trash can. I ain't a dang mind reader.

Now, y'all are gonna find as you read on in this book that no topic is too taboo, no problem is too small, and no dilemma is too personal for me to tackle. Why, I answer questions that Dear Abby would've backed away from, and maybe I should have too, but y'all are my fans. Y'all write and say how you love me like I was a cousin, and so I felt that I had to try and take on even the questions that no one else would dare touch. I had to risk my career and good standin' in my community to try and deal with the hard issues as well, regardless if they were situations that I even found repulsive. So y'all are gonna come across topics that I've never discussed in any of my other four books, but since I felt that they affect us all, I just had to include them. An example of this would be the letter I got from the mother who can't stop her littlest one from peein' in the bathtub when she gives her and her sisters a bath. Now you won't find that subject matter in my BBQin' cookbook, I can tell you that. Or then there's the gal who is tired of bein' cheated on as well as bein' single, and so she wants to know if it's wrong to date a prisoner just for the security of knowin' where he is late at night. Again, another example of a subject that you ain't gonna find even in my *Livin' Real Good* book.

Let me say here and now that, as some of y'all have pointed out from time to time, I ain't had no higher learnin'. I didn't study with professors in some fancy college or university. I also ain't read one of them great big books that they don't carry at my local library by Sigmund Fraud or Freud or whatever the fella's name was where they blame all your problems on somebody else. My degrees in this field come from the school of Hard Knocks, the college of Kicked in the Teeth, and the university of What the Heck Happened. Yes, my advice comes from hands-on learnin', if you know what I mean, and tryin' to keep your head above the water.

So as you read on, I hope that y'all will find the answers that you might be lookin' for through the well-thought-out and practical solutions that I share. And I got a feelin' that this one is gonna be a hard one for y'all to put down, especially with all the wisdom that I've imparted in these pages. For many of y'all this book is gonna be the light at the end of the tunnel, or the flotation device to life that's in some ways similar to that airplane seat cushion that you might be sittin' on right now as you read this. And for others, it will simply be a sort of daily guidepost that they can lean on each mornin' when they wake up to their real world. Regardless, I know that this book is gonna change a lot of your lives for the better and give you a boost to better livin' like you never had before. But whatever you do, don't hog it all. No, dear readers, share what you've learned from me with others. Show them the way to gettin' over their problems. Give this book to everyone you know. Don't be a tightwad. Go to your favorite bookstore or jump online and order copies of this guide of knowledge for everyone that you love, like, or just plain old know. You can make a difference in their lives, and me and this book will do all the work for you, but you've got to get it in their hands.

Oh, and one last thing. Keep them cards, letters, and e-mails in English comin', 'cause I'm always there for you, I want to do all I can to make your lives easier, and I might need more material for a second advice book! God bless!

Love, Kisses, and Trailer Park Wishes,
Ruby Ann Boxcar
rubylot18@aol.com
www.rubyannboxcar.com

The Residents of the High Chaparral Trailer Park, Lot by Lot

As you can see, Night Skate is doin' great down at the Rinky Dink Roller Rink.

I do declare that since we last spoke, the cold weather has brought on nothin' but madness at the High Chaparral Trailer Park. Well, that's a lie. It's also brought on job promotions, love, and even soon-to-be-weddin's. Of course there was also a little bit of sorrow with a passin' amongst us. And we can't forget the excitin' changes that have taken place down at the Rinky Dink Roller Rink as well as the R.U. Inn, but we'll get into that later. Why, just in the last few months, the High Chaparral has turned out to be a little Peyton Place—without the class and the good clothes.

On the subject of weddin's, we've had three planned, with a fourth one that, as you read on will see, had to be dropped, to take place on the same day, June 21. Now these brides didn't pick that date on account of it bein' my husband's birthday, but rather 'cause it's the first day of summer and it falls on a Monday, which means everybody in attendance can get off an extra day from work. The funny thing was that none of the engaged had talked to the other couples about it when they was settin' their dates. It just worked out that way. Seein' how they all belong to the same Baptist church, there was bound to be a problem with who got the use of the church and when, not to mention the scheduled rehearsal time. Well, you can only imagine the mean-spirited bickerin' that was takin' place over somethin' that was supposed to be so special. It got so bad that finally Pastor Ida May Bee, bein' the religious leader that she is, told the couples to sit down, take a pill, shut up, and listen 'cause she was gonna tell 'em how it'd be, and if they didn't like it, then they could just up and try and find somebody else that was as close

3

to God as she is to do their weddin's. She went on to tell 'em that there was no way she was gonna conduct three ceremonies on the same day in the middle of June in that hot box of a church. After all, the little window air-conditionin' units that are in there now are lucky to keep it cool enough for her Sunday service, let alone three to five hours' worth of weddin' services. And not only that, but Pastor Ida May Bee made it very clear that Mondays, especially those that fall between June and August, were her days off from bein' a pillar of the community and God's right-hand woman. Even the good Lord above rested one day, and even on that day she has to work. So if all those couples were dead set for a Monday weddin', then it would be a triple ceremony in an air-conditioned area where she, the guests, and family members weren't herded up like cattle on their way to market. And even though she'd only be doin' one ceremony, she'd still be expectin' to get paid for three. After all, if they want a cheap weddin', then they could go have a Unitarian minister perform the service. Well, these three couples took Pastor Ida May's lecture to heart and decided that she was right. If they wanted a nice weddin', then they'd all have to work together like the good neighbors that they were. Within weeks the arrangements were approved and the invitations went out. There is one couple whose invites do say that they are "upon approval of the bride's mother," which y'all will shortly understand.

In any case, this next June the services will be held on Monday the 21st at Lamb's Super Store followed by a reception for couple number one at Papa Lamb's Pizza located in the back of the store, a reception for couple number two at the Taco Tackle Shack North, and a reception for couple number three at the Vance Pool Funeral Center. As far as the actual ceremony itself, chairs will be set up in the front of the store for guests and family. Couple one will come down Aisle 4, while couple two make their way down Aisle 7, and couple three comes down Aisle 10 all at the same time. They'll then join together around the end caps of Aisles 8, 7, and 9. Pastor Ida May Bee, who will be standin' directly in front of the candy stand in the 7 ITEMS OR LESS checkout lane, will conduct the service over the store intercom with Nellie Tinkle playin' an in-house electric keyboard back in the electronics department. After each couple has said their "I do's" they will get in line at the checkout counters in front of them, and pay for the pastor's fees with either cash, credit card, or a personal check as long as they have a second form of ID. Once each bride and groom provides a receipt of payment, they will be pronounced "man and wife." It really should be pretty, even though the store will remain open for business durin' the whole thing. But hey, they got air-conditionin'.

I guess all I can say is thank goodness the rest of the year will be much brighter, especially when this August they put in that water treatment plant like I told you about in my last book. I got a feelin' there's gonna be a lot of tanned people here at the High Chaparral Trailer Park.

Lot #1

Trust me when I tell y'all that you're gonna want to set down for this one. Just this past March, dog-ugly Opal Lamb-Inman, who along with her momma, Dottie, owns Lamb's Super Store, pulled the shag carpet out from underneath us by announcin' that she was leavin' her husband of one and a half years, Dick Inman. Actually she'd given him his walkin' papers along with the two male servants and a high six-figure settlement and told him to get out. Now I know that most of y'all who've read one of my past books are havin' to pick yourselves up off the floor at this point in time. Actually Opal said that she and Dick remain friends although he was extremely upset about her wantin' a divorce and all, but when she told him that she wasn't leavin' him out of hatred, and that she planned on givin' him a very large amount of money for the trouble, "he lit up like a little schoolgirl." He packed his bags, signed the divorce papers, cashed the check, and moved to Little Rock with his maid, Uri, and his butler, Buck. As far as his law office, he just turned the whole thing over to my niece, Lulu Bell, who owns the property. Y'all will recall that he'd gone in and fixed up the backroom area and even put rooms with cots in them as well as installin' TVs, a sauna room, and a hot tub. Lulu Bell says that her boyfriend, Billy Bob, who's quite the businessman, thinks she ought to forget about rentin' it and instead turn it into a workout facility or maybe a YMCA.

Of course many of us at the High Chaparral Trailer Park thought Opal had lost her mind when we first heard the news. After all, she was lucky to have a man in the first place bein' as ugly as sin as you can be and still go into a Baptist church. Dick, on the other hand, wasn't a bad-lookin' man, and he was a lawyer to boot. But we all thought that if anybody was gonna leave anybody, it would've been Dick that would have left Opal. Just think about it. Wakin' up next to her in the mornin' would make Frankenstein's monster holler in fear. But we was all wrong. Opal will agree that she was lucky to have Dick, but it wasn't until a recent trip that she realized she had never really been in love with him.

Back in February, she and Dick went to Hollywood for a Valentine's Day vacation. Now if you've ever been to Hollywood then you know how romantic the place can be with all them hills and palm trees and such. Of course, unlike Opal and Dick, I think I'd have left my two male servants, if I had any, at home. And even if I had brung 'em with me, I certainly wouldn't have booked 'em in a different hotel. Poor Dick was havin' to run back and forth in his rental car several times of the day and night just to make sure that they was OK. Opal says that sometimes the poor thing was so tired from the trips that he didn't trust himself to stay awake while drivin' back to join her in their hotel room, so he just slept over with Uri and Buck. I can tell you what, I sure wouldn't have been sleepin' on a hard hotel room floor while my butler and maid were sleepin' in a king-size bed shaped like a heart. But of course, that's just me. Well, anyways, I guess everythin' was goin' just fine on the trip. And then they took that Warner Brothers studio tour. It was on that tour that some man came chasin' after the oversize golf cart that you and ten to twelve other folks ride around the sets in, yellin' for it to stop. At first Opal and Dick thought it was some kind of show that they did for all the tour guests. But then when this guy, who was desperately tryin' to catch his breath, came up to Opal and said how unique her beauty was, Dick knew that either somethin' was up or the fella had forgotten to take his medication before comin' to work.

Well, as it turned out, this guy was a makeup artist by the name of Ryan Brown who specialized in horror makeup, and he wanted to do a model of Opal's face. Dick said it would be fine, and seein' how it could take half the day, he and his staff left Opal and Ryan at the studio. That was Dick's first mistake. Menfolk out there, listen to me now. If some fella comes up to your wife, regardless of how dirt ugly she might be, and tells her how beautiful she is, don't leave her with him. I don't care if he's uglier than she is, don't do it. After all, there is one thing a woman likes better than a sexy husband, and that's a man who makes her feel special. And this is what Ryan did to Opal. He kept goin' on about how attractive she was and how if she was his girl he'd want to be with her all the time. Opal swears that he was sayin' this to her even before he'd stuck two straws up her nose and covered her face in plaster, which by the way, they had to do twice since the first time the stuff wouldn't form around her face. Ryan said he'd never seen that happen before, but the next time they had no problem. Mind you, they had to shut the lights off first. Anyways, before Ryan sent her home, and Opal could actually get a cab to stop for her, she had fallen in love with him. Opal kept it to herself for two days. Part of that was the fact that Dick didn't make it back to the room for that amount of time, but when he did get back, she sat him down and confessed her feelin's. And once Opal had taken out her checkbook and given him a down payment on the settlement money that she had promised, he got on his cell phone and called the studio in an attempt to locate Ryan for her.

Anyways, long story short, Ryan felt the same way about Opal, and now with the divorce gone through, they're seein' each other. We all hope this long-distance relationship works out. When he's workin' she spends each weekend with him in L.A., and when he's off he spends his time with her at the High Chaparral Trailer Park. He's a real nice guy, and very handsome as well. And you can tell that he really, really loves her. The way he showers her with affection is really romantic if you can stand to look at it. And even though they kiss and hug and hold hands like folks half their age, which would honestly gross out a moose, Opal still says that she has refused to allow Ryan to make a cast of her body until after they've wed. Ryan has asked for Dottie's blessin', and even though she promises to give it, Opal's momma says she'll only give the OK for the weddin' after a two-month waitin' period from the divorce date has passed. After all, she don't want nobody to think that her daughter, Opal, is a tramp. We all assured Dottie that no one would ever think that, but she still insists on waitin' till June. That means that Opal will be a June bride since they plan on marryin' just as soon as Dottie says they can. As a matter of fact, Opal and Ryan have already set a date of June 21, as I told y'all at the start of this section, after gettin' a little wink from Dottie. Needless to say, as you'll soon learn after readin' a little further on, she won't be the only June bride in the trailer park. Let's just hope that this time around the flowers in Opal's bouquet don't wilt in her hand like they did at her last weddin'. And who knows if after Opal and Ryan get hitched they will turn their trailer park in Lot #1 into their main home, or if they will just move to Hollywood. I guess we'll have to wait on that one. Best of luck to both of y'all!

Lot #2

Anita Biggon, my old childhood friend, is doin' real good. As y'all will recall, I told you in my last book, *Ruby Ann's Down Home Trailer Park Guide to Livin' Real Good,* that Anita had installed them portable walls in her new place, Anita's Bar and Grill, so she could block off the bar durin' lunchtime. This was so good Baptist folks like Sister Bertha could come in and eat without havin' to worry about people thinkin' they was sinnin'. Well, that really drove up her lunch business to the point that she ran out of seatin' room and needed to build on to the place. The only problem was that Larry's Construction, who Anita had paid in full to build the addition, had to delay all their projects on account of their entire construction team bein' arrested and sent back to Mexico, leavin' Larry to do all the work himself. And since nobody in these parts with a valid social security card and second form of ID will work and supply their own tools for $2 an hour, it looks like it might be a whole year before Anita's Bar and Grill gets any bigger. So Anita was forced to take other actions to help out with her dinin' room dilemma. She bought twelve foldin' table-and-chair sets from Lamb's Super Store and set 'em out front of her place, creatin' a rather nice outside-café look. Why, when the wind is blowin' the right way so as you can't smell the nearby hog farm located across the highway by the Rinky Dink Roller Rink, you'd swear you was havin' lunch at one of them fancy cafés in Paris. Needless to say, the first couple of days the outside dinin' was great, and business was boomin'. But then some teenage thugs got the bright idea, while out from school on a lunch break, to wait around the block until Anita had got all the tables and chairs put up. Then they'd peel out and run their cars right through the middle of the outside café. Since no one had taken a seat outside yet, nobody was hurt, but most of the chairs and tables were busted up and strewn all over the place, makin' Anita have to race out to buy more.

This continued every day for a week. Finally Anita demanded that Sheriff Gentry do somethin' about it. Of course he claimed that since no one had actually gotten the license plate number since it was covered up with some kind of cloth, there was nothin' he could do. But if y'all know Anita, she ain't one to take no for an answer. So she talked the sheriff into comin' over to her bar and grill for a free lunch. She waited until he had got to the restaurant and then after he'd helped himself to the buffet, she took him outside and set up a table and one chair for him to use. Well, no sooner had she unfolded that chair than this 1977 maroon Malibu came tearin' around the corner and drove right towards the now seated Sheriff Gentry. Luckily he saw it comin', so he dove out of the way as it obliviated the open-air dinin' area. As you can guess, Anita's plan had convinced the sheriff to take action. So now every day at

10:50 you'll find Sheriff Gentry up on top the roof with his high-powered rifle and a fresh plate filled with items from the buffet below. Once the word got out that he would be up there every day at lunch, aimin' to shoot out the tires or windshields of any vehicle that tried to drive through the outdoor patio of Anita's Bar and Grill, the vandalism stopped. There was the one incident when Momma Ballzak got a little too close to the yellow line in the middle of the street while on her way to work at the R.U. Inn, and Sheriff Gentry opened fire on her. If you've ever seen Sheriff Gentry shoot a firearm, then you know that he missed her car completely, but did hit a treetop, 'causin' a large branch to come crashin' down onto the street directly in front of Momma Ballzak's car. This in turn made her swerve to the right, runnin' her into the one pump they got at Al's Stop and Pump Gas Station. Luckily Momma Ballzak was able to put the car in reverse and back up to a safe distance before the pump blew sky high. I tell you, the blast alone shattered windows all around, and knocked Al Hornpucker clean through the back door of his business. As fate would have it, no one was injured, and not an outside chair or table over at Anita's was damaged.

Lot #3

Even though they still got some of the best Tex-Mex this side of the Mississippi, both the Taco Tackle Shack and the Taco Tackle Shack North have lost some of their lunch crowd to Anita's Bar and Grill. Now, don't get me wrong, they still pull in a good afternoon business for those customers that are cravin' a great big greasy Frito chili pie or a mouth-waterin' cheese-stuffed chile relleño. But now when you head in at around noon at either location, you're almost sure to find an empty seat, or table for that matter. And Lois and Hubert Bunch both know that you can't compete with good American food like what they're servin' up at Anita's. But they also know that in time folks will eventually get that old hankerin' that they used to have at lunchtime for a taquito or a hand-rolled tamale with Hubert's very own chili con queso sauce. And with the money they bring in for dinner, especially when they got them cliff divers and water-skiers performin', they can make it without a big lunch crowd. And after all, their good neighbor Anita has promised that she will not serve anythin' Mexican soundin' from 11:00 A.M. to 1:30 P.M. In return, Lois and Hubert have said that they'd take apple pie off their menu completely, which to be honest wasn't no great loss.

Dear Ruby Ann

With the success of the revamped nighttime entertainment, the blindfolded skiin' Chihuahuas now appearin' on Tuesdays and Fridays at the original Taco Tackle Shack and the midget cliff divers doin' their thing on Wednesday and Thursday at the Taco Tackle Shack North, the Bunches have decided to expand their south-of-the-border food business even more. As y'all know, the beautiful state of Arkansas has over six hundred thousand acres of some of the most gorgeously clear lakes you've ever seen. We get folks from all parts of the country comin' to our state to fish, boat, scuba dive, and just about anything else that's water related. Well, one night Lois couldn't sleep 'cause Hubert was snorin' like an elephant with a head cold. Finally reachin' the point where she couldn't take no more, she poked him in his side and told him to roll over. To this the sleepin' Hubert replied, "Hang on, I've almost caught this one, but I'm too hungry." He then rolled over, and Lois jumped up screamin' his name. Hubert sprang out of that bed like somebody had put lit matches between his toes. At first he was madder than a Democrat at a Florida vote count, but when Lois told Hubert that she had an idea for a new business, he quickly overcame his anger. Accordin' to Lois, all these people who come out every year to play or fish in the lakes have to eat, too. And since the lake property is so expensive to purchase and then put up a restaurant, why not just bring the food to them? So before you could say "anchors aweigh" Hubert had bought four of them flat-bottomed johnboats that can skim across the water regardless of how deep or shallow it might be, and had 'em covered with a fiberglass shell. In the meantime Lois had found cigarette lighters that could be adapted to boat motors as well as these portable mini refrigerator/warmers that plug into the cigarette lighter, thus keepin' your cold items cold and your hot items hot. After hirin' on a four-person crew, one for each mini restaurant, Lois and Hubert filled up the portable fridge/warmers with selections from their limited menu, loaded up a cooler filled with all kinds of pop, put the chest with the assorted bait on board as well, and put their "roach boats" out on a few lakes. These floatin' chimichangas, which is what they were shaped like, were quite a hit. At first folks didn't know what to think when they saw a bobbin' Mexican food item barrelin' towards 'em at high speed with "La Cucaracha" blastin' from its onboard speakers, but within time they eventually got used to this sight. And as you can guess, Lois's late-night idea was a happy sight to all who could now just continue with their water activities and still enjoy lunch.

The only problem that they encountered was with the name for these portable Taco Tackle Shacks. Hubert wanted to let folks out in the water know that this was part of the Taco Tackle Shack, but it would have taken up the entire fiberglass chimichanga to put that on it so folks could make it out from a distance. So instead he decided on just droppin' "the Shack" part all together and simply usin' the capital "T" from "Taco" as well at the capital "T" from "Tackle." This would fit on the boat shells without any problem, and folks could see 'em from several yards away. But then Lois said that folks needed to know that just 'cause the hoverin' water cafés were small, the taste of the food was just as good as you'd get at any of the Taco Tackle Shack locations. So in order to express this message, they changed the name, and by Friday of the second week there were four giant chimichangas floatin' around the lake with the words "BIG T.T.s" written across 'em in great big black letters. As you might have guessed, by Saturday the holes that folks had made by throwin' things at the boats had been patched up, the Bunches slapped on a fresh coat of paint and repainted the words "Food Shack" on 'em before settin' out on the lake for business. And of course, the request for the employees to be allowed to carry firearms and mace was totally rejected.

Just before I turned this book into the publisher, I spoke with Lois, and she says that they've got twelve more Food Shacks bein' prepared even now. This time they'll resemble both hard and soft tacos, tamales, two cheese enchiladas, and other Tex-Mex items. I'd kill to be a fly on the wall when them foreign spy planes report in after flyin' over prairie county and tell their government officials that the Americans got a giant sopapia floatin' out on Peckerwood Lake. They're gonna think them boys are crazier than my sister after drinkin' a bottle of rubbin' alcohol.

Congratulations to Lois and Hubert and their new business.

Lot #4

You know, it was really nice for Nellie Tinkle and her husband to open their trailer doors to dear old Wendy Bottom a few years back. As those of you who've read *Ruby Ann's Down Home Trailer Park Holiday Cookbook* will recall, Wendy had always wanted to learn how to play the organ, and with the passin' of her husband, Harry Bottom, the then eighty-nine-year-old decided that now was as good a time as any. And here we are, almost two years later, and Wendy's talents on the organ are phenomenal. Of course there are occasions when she gets lost in the sheet music and it ends up soundin' more like a frightened cat with its tail caught in the keyboard than a good old-fashioned Baptist hymn, but for the most part, she really does play well. And this is most likely why Nellie offered her a partnership in the new business she's decided to start up. You see, with the way that the world is today, there are lots of tent revivals springin' up left and right, and these camp meetin's need organists. Well, since the services are held on week nights, and Pastor Ida May Bee has given Nellie her blessin' to play for these folks just as long as no snakes are involved, Nellie has decided to join forces with Wendy to fill these positions. As you can guess, most of these evangelists would give their eyeteeth to have either one of these gals runnin' their fingers across their organs. So Nellie and Wendy are fufillin' their needs by openin' the Tinkle-Bottom Society. Of course they've added a few other piano and organ players as well to their new company, but Wendy and Nellie, who now has lots of free time after what happened at the Rinky Dink Roller Rink (see Lot #9), are both playin' under the big tents practically every night of the week. And C.M. drops 'em all off at each revival in the area and then goes back to his trailer and waits by the phone. Both Nellie and Wendy, as well as the other musicians that they hire to play the keys, all have cell phones with the speed dial set to ring Lot #4. They've all been instructed to jump on the phone if they hear the slightest rattle or hissin' come up from the pulpit, and C.M. will race over and pick 'em up. So far so good, thank the Lord. Both Nellie and Wendy seem pretty happy with the whole business arrangement just as long as C.M. remembers to TiVo all their wrestlin' shows.

Lot #5

I've got good news. Momma finally gave up her job as a pizza delivery driver for Papa Lamb's Pizza. Even though we're all a little disappointed 'cause we lost our pizza discounts, the family is glad to know that she's at home durin' the night, and not in the back of some taxi cab droppin' off pizzas to strangers' homes. But y'all will never guess what she's doin' now. My momma has become a model! Who would have ever thought? Well, to be honest, she did do a little modelin' for some local ads back when Wards was still around, but she never did anythin' like she's doin' now. It seems that the president of this company spotted her photo in my last book and instantly knew she would be perfect for his company. I guess he contacted my publisher and then they called her and passed on his message. Well, one thing led to another and now Momma is the official print model for one of them emergency necklaces buttons that you push when you need help. She just loves it. Of course that is most likely 'cause she gets to lay around on the job if you know what I mean. She is also their hand model for medical ID bracelets. Once a month either me or my sister, Donna Sue, drive Momma over to a photo studio in Conway so they can do the pictures for the next month's ads. She really is pretty good, and when the photographer cues her, she gets this painful look on her face that resembles the one on most folks after they've seen my sister, Donna Sue, naked. And it don't look like Momma's fame is gonna stop here. Oh, no sir, she just was in Little Rock auditionin' for a commercial for a very popular antacid. Who knows, today it could be medical alert buttons, and tomorrow, if she's lucky, it could be the ever-coveted hemorrhoid cream TV spots.

As for Daddy, well, he is doin' just fine. They've moved him from greeter at Lamb's Super Store, all the way up to outside security, which means he spends all day drivin' around the parkin' lot in that golf cart. And with Daddy at the wheel, you can understand why they had to add big foam bumpers all around the cart. He hasn't hit anyone yet, thank goodness, but he did chase down a shoplifter. He went almost a whole mile until the battery ran out, and then Daddy pursued the fella on foot. The police said he would've most likely caught him, too, if the wheel on Daddy's walker hadn't locked up. After that incident, Daddy started carryin' a baseball bat in his golf cart. Of course, as soon as Dottie Lamb found out about the bat she made Daddy put it back in the sportin' goods department 'cause she was afraid that someone might sue her over it. So now, with her permission, Daddy carries a badge, a walkie-talkie, and a brand-new top-of-the-line badminton racket. So when you stop by Lamb's Super Store, keep your nose clean—'cause Daddy's got a wicked smash swing.

Lot #6

In my mind as well as hers, my dear sister, Donna Sue, has always been a star. Of course she's been a star in the world of professional exotic dancin', even nowadays in her late fifties. But with the recent release of her book, *Donna Sue's Down Home Trailer Park Bartending Guide,* this overweight siblin' of mine is takin' the stage nightly at the

Blue Whale Strip Club to thunderin' applause and utter excitement. Why, I even hear that when she dances, people are actually tippin' her with whole dollar bills now instead of loose change, foreign currency, and fast-food coupons. Needless to say, I couldn't be happier for her, especially when you consider the terrible events that have taken place since her book came out.

In my *Livin' Real Good* book I told y'all that Donna Sue had been seein' seventy-four-year-old highway watermelon stand/Christmas tree lot baron Buford Pits. Well, this past Halloween, at the High Chaparral Trailer Park's Mother in-Law's Day/Halloween party, Buford got down on one knee in front of my momma and asked her if she'd do him the honor. Of course at first all of us thought he'd blown a nut in that brain of his and was askin' Momma to be his bride. Well, before Daddy could get to his feet via his custom-made lawn chair with the liftin' cushion that me and Dew got him for his birthday, Buford went on and said that he'd like her to do him the honor of bein' his mother-in-law. I don't know if it was 'cause she was so excited that her oldest daughter was finally gettin' married or the fact that his old bony knee was on her foot, but she yelled yes just as soon as he was finished askin' the question. With that answer, some of the fellas lifted Buford off the ground and softly placed him in front of Daddy, who'd quickly calmed down by this time.

"You know, Mr. Boxcar, I'm an old-fashioned man," Buford said, "which is why I'd like to ask you for your daughter's hand in marriage."

"Well, Buford," Daddy replied, "I'm afraid that you're gonna have to take that fat behind of hers as well as the rest of her in marriage too." Leave it to Daddy to try and get the last laugh. But old Buford outdid him by sayin' that he'd take all of her just as long as he didn't have to try and pick her up. Needless to say, we was all in tears by then from laughin'. And it was romantic, too, in a sort of *Twilight Zone* kind of way. Naturally, Daddy went on to give his blessin', and then them menfolk picked Buford back up and rested him down in front of Donna Sue.

"Pardon me," Buford said to my blushin' sister, "but, Hot Pants, will you marry me?" Hot Pants was the nickname that he gave Donna Sue after she'd mistakenly set down on one of them standin' ashtrays on their first date. It wasn't until five minutes later when they smelled somethin' that resembled the odor of a couch on fire that they realized a smolderin' cigarette had started her capri pants to blazin'.

My sister looked him straight in the eye and said, "That depends, old man. Can I still dance and keep all my businesses if I say yes?"

"I wouldn't have it any other way, Hot Pants."

"Well, then call your lawyer and change your will, 'cause you got your-self a wife," my sister replied back. As you can guess, once they were able to get Buford's leg stretched back out, he and my sister started hug-gin' and kissin', which of course turned our stomachs to no end. Regard-less, we were happy for both of 'em. And it was the next day that they announced their weddin' date for June 21. Finally my sister had found love, and no form of liquor was involved, well, except on his part.

A few weeks later, my sister and Buford hitched her patented Wienies on Wheels Wagon up to the back of her Bonneville and they headed up to Wisconsin so she could demonstrate it to a group of folks who were interested in buyin' a few franchises. After all, nothin' goes better with a hot wienie than cold beer, so where better than Wisconsin to have some of Donna Sue's very own Wienies on Wheels Wagons. Well, the meetin' went great and before they left to go back to their motel, my sister had signed on five new Wienies on Wheels. That night as she and Buford went to bed nothin' was in her mind but business. All she'd have to do now was go back home, deposit their checks, and once they cleared, call Verland over at his weldin' shop and have him put the order of custom-designed wagons together. Of course when she awoke the next day, business would be the last thing on her mind.

It wasn't until Donna Sue was fixin' her hair that she realized Buford was dead. At first she thought he'd just fallen back to sleep after a little bit of early mornin' passions, but as she would later find out, her husband-to-be had actually died in his sleep sometime durin' the night. Well, after the police and coroner had given her the OK, she contacted the funeral home to make arrangements for shippin' the body of the man she loved back to Arkansas for burial. Needless to say, she about had a heart at-tack herself when she heard how much it was gonna cost. So instead, she just threw a few bags of ice in her Wienies on Wheels Wagon, loaded Buford up, and drove him back to the High Chaparral Trailer Park herself. Since she was the nearest thing to family that the poor old man had, she took care of the funeral and all, and buried the love of her life. As it turned out, Buford left her everythin', includin' his highway stands. So she sold off his house, bought her a double wide, and put armed guards around her highway Christmas tree lots at night this past holiday season.

Did I mention that she's back to her old datin' ways again? Of course she will never forget dear old Buford Pits. As a matter of fact, she had his dentures made into a staple remover, which she proudly displays on the desk in her trailer home office.

Lot #7

Pastor Ida May Bee is up in arms over the recent restrictions to the church Web site. As y'all recall, in my last book I told y'all that she'd decided not to do online baptisms anymore since that one fella almost electrocuted himself when his laptop fell into the bathtub with him. Well, since then she's had to stop doin' online Communion since the state said that she couldn't sell the grape drink boxes and Ritz crackers online without a food license. Needless to say, she was fit to be tied. So instead of bowin' down to "the man," she has just pulled them services from the Web page and has revamped the whole thing. You can still become an online member of the Holier Than Most Baptist Church, but at this time you can't participate in the actual services. You can still get T-shirts and other items that say you're a member, and even read some of Pastor Ida May's thoughts on daily livin'. Just go to my Web site at *www.rubyannboxcar.com* and click on the Church link on the lower-left-hand side of the page.

As you well know, Pastor Ida had been doin' a lot of travelin' all across this fine country of ours, bein' a livin' example of saintliness. Some of y'all have probably met her as well, and have enjoyed speakin' with her on many topics. Why, I even hear she has personally tried to show the love of her faith to several lost souls durin' her public appearances over the past year. And now she has decided to take some of us church members along with her on the trips she makes this year. Needless to say, we're about as tickled as a pig in mud to go with her. As a matter of fact, even as I put pen to paper, I'm mentally decidin' what to wear on our upcomin' trip to Paris, Texas. We're gonna make a pilgrimage to see the monument in the Evergreen Cemetery that they got of Jesus wearin' a pair of cowboy boots. Even though none of us has ever actually seen the statue before, I am told, disappointingly, that it don't depict the scene where our Savior kicked the moneychangers out of the temple. That would have made for a good monument or even a wonderful velvet paintin' where Jesus and the Duke are throwin' 'em out. I might just have to have that one commissioned and then donate it to the church. Anyways, I know that the trip will be fun and inspirational with Pastor Ida May Bee and Brother Woody Bee leadin' the way, regardless of how the cowboy-booted Jesus is posed or if he's kickin' the devil out of somebody or not.

Lot #8

My niece, Lulu Bell Boxcar, as well as her boyfriend and now fiancé, Billy Bob Buttons, are the couple number two that I spoke of in the openin' of this chapter. They were given the state's approval to marry last year like I told y'all about, which was somethin' they had to do since they both had ridden a small bus to school when they was little, if you catch my drift. Anyways, as you already read, they finally set their weddin' date. Lulu Bell has been goin' nuts about everything from her weddin' dress to the reception music, so finally I had to just step in and calm her down. I set her down one afternoon at her kitchen table, and she and I went over everythin' that she and Billy Bob would need for the weddin'. Now if y'all have been followin' along with me in my past books, you know that these kids ain't doin' bad financially. As a matter of fact, with all the money they make off of their businesses and rental properties, they do better than me, if you can believe that. So when it came to plannin' everythin' out, money was not in any way an issue. The problem was tryin' to get these two kids, who in actuality are both in their thirties, to decided on somethin' sensible. For example, Lulu Bell wanted her weddin' dress to be yellow, purple, red, and lime green, the colors of her favorite TV stars, the Teletubbies. And Billy Bob wanted an orange tux with the hat like he saw in the movie *Dumb and Dumber.* Thank goodness at least one of 'em has some taste when it comes to special-event clothes. I had to tell Lulu Bell that her dress had to be white since it was her first weddin', but if she really wanted the Teletubbies to play a part in her weddin' then she could have 'em on her weddin' cake. She finally agreed to that, which was the best news I'd heard since mortician Vance Pool told me that his tuxedo shop in the basement of the funeral home had enough orange outfits to fit the groom and the best men. My husband, Dew, who'll be walkin' her down the aisle, will be usin' his own orange tux.

Lot #9

The Rinky Dink Roller Rink has become an even bigger success recently. They now have a skate night on Thursdays that is completely new and original. Bein' the world traveler that I am, I've got to say that I've never seen anythin' like it before. What happens is that when you rent your pair of skates, you also get one of them foam sumo wrestler outfits and a bike helmet at no additional charge. When children rent their skates, they are given a pillowcase with a little head hole at the top and two arm holes in the side along with a bag of pillow or couch stuffin', a rope, and a child's bike helmet. Then right at 7:00 P.M. Harland closes the curtains and shuts off the lights for what he calls "Night Skate." That's right, nobody can see who's in front of or directly behind 'em.

Juanita, who works weekends only at the Piggly Wiggly now, says that she and her husband, Harland, came up with the idea after the power blew on a Monday night. "It was so exciting for both the few skaters that were here that evening as well as for the staff. Since the organ had gone out as well, Nellie Tinkle just continued the live music on her kazoo. Everyone had a ball during those ten minutes of darkness." Juanita runs the concession stand at the Rinky Dink Roller Rink.

"It's kind of like bumper cars without the car," Harland claims. "And it's fun that the entire family can enjoy. It gets so hectic out there on the skatin' rink that we had to put up blacked-out Plexiglas walls around the organ just so patrons don't get knocked on top of Nellie Tinkle as she plays her music to skate by." Nellie does have a pen light that shines on her sheet music, but other than the dimmed lights in the concession stand, it's black as night in the Rinky Dink Roller Rink on Thursday evenin's.

And the good news is that the Hix family are doin' so well that they can finally get braces for their little girl Bonita Hix. God bless her, that child could open a can with them buckteeth of hers. Heck, she could eat corn through a chain-link fence. Why, you'd swear that little thing had beaver in her. But the dentist says that her teeth will be just like normal in about eighteen to twenty years.

Lot #10

With all the trials and tribulations dear old former school cafeteria worker Ollie White has gone through over the years, it was amazin' to us to see that she still has her faith, or so we thought. Ollie has never missed a Sunday at the Holier Than Most Baptist Church, which she and her late husband, Orville, joined as youngsters more than fifty years ago. But still, I guess the straw that unbeknownst to us broke the camel's back in her religious life was losin' her job at the school cafeteria, which I talked about in my *Livin' Real Good* book. She was so upset that she just threw her hands up to the whole church thing. Of course she still attended Sunday services regularly. After all, you ain't got to love the Lord or even believe in him for that matter to attend church on a regular basis. But in her mind, if he wasn't there for her when she'd needed him, then why should she allow him into her heart. Well, when Ollie came wobblin' down the aisle durin' Pastor Ida May Bee's usual end-of-the-service altar call, you should have heard the gasps of disbelief. Of course we're all supposed to have our eyes closed durin' this part of the service, but bein' the good Baptists that we are, we always keep one of 'em squinted so we can see which sinner we don't have to try and covert every time we talk to 'em.

Ollie White confessed her wicked ways that mornin', voluntarily out loud, and said that she wanted to rededicate her life right there and then. She also said that she wanted all of us to forgive her for "wanderin' off from the flock." To that Pastor Ida May Bee put her arms around the old woman and told her that as long as she didn't bring any social diseases back with her, she was welcomed back into our flock just as if she'd never lost her way. Well, that brought tears to all our eyes. Pastor Ida May has such a way with words. I often think that she would make a good writer as well.

The followin' Sunday after church we all went down to the river so Ollie could be rebaptized. Of course, we believe that once you've been baptized you ain't got to do it again, but since it is also an outward sign of your faith, Ollie White insisted that she go through the whole submersion as part of her rededicatin' her life, which was our honor as her friends and fellow members of the church to attend. Even though we've got a baptismal tank, Ollie said that she wanted to do it the same way she'd done it when she'd been baptized as a teenager, out in the lake. She had originally wanted to even do it in the same location where as a young girl she'd been dunked under, but that part of the lake was so overrun with water moccasins that Pastor Ida May told her she'd "have to join the Pentecostal Holiness church if she wanted to be baptized in them waters." So Ollie settled just to renew her baptism in a safer section of the lake.

Ollie, wearin' an old dress, carefully made her way out into the cold February lake water with assistance from Brother Woody Bee, the pastor's husband. Then with all of us witnessin' her rededication, Pastor Ida May Bee prayed over her and then gently leaned her back into the water. And that was when things got weird. Ollie's legs started kickin' and her hands were flappin' in the water as if she was drownin'.

"I need some help out here," Pastor Ida May Bee yelled up towards the shore. Within seconds Brother Woody Bee had reached his wife and began tryin' to help her lift Ollie out of the water. Finally, as Ollie came rushin' out of the lake, a scream of terror came over all the ladies of the church. You see, somehow Ollie White had managed to noodle a sixty-six-pound catfish while she was under. In other words, for all you non-fishin' readers out there, Ollie had caught a sixty-six-pound catfish with nothin' more than just her head. None of us had ever seen a fish that big before, let alone a catfish caught with a person's head. All I can figure is it must of been the Aqua Net. Of course several of the menfolk who'd jumped into the water when Pastor Ida May Bee had hollered for assistance, lead Ollie up to the shore before gettin' that catfish off her head. After all, it'd almost be a sin to let that baby get back into the water. Plus, it was a miracle. The good book says that we'd be "fishers of men," and right before our eyes Ollie White had done somethin' kind of like

From left to right: Pastor Ida May Bee, catfish, Ollie White, and Brother Woody Bee.

that. Our dearly loved sister in the church had come back to the flock and the good Lord had given us a reason to have a fish fry all on the same day. Even though I don't like fish, I still had a nice time at the impromptu gatherin', 'cause I was blessed as well that day. You see, my husband, Dew, had thought to bring his camera, so I had a good photo for this book.

Lot #11

There's nothin' much goin' on with Kitty and Kyle lately except for the new additions to Kitty's convenience store, Gas and Smokes. If you recall I told y'all in my last book that Kitty had added one new tannin' bed over by where the video games area is, and it looked like she might add a second bed in there as well. I was right. Now she has a full tannin' facility right there in Gas and Smokes, which means you can either lay down on the new bed and get a tan or you can stand up and tan. She didn't get a third unit, it's just that one of the front legs on the first bed broke off, causin' it to tilt. Well, they tried installing a seat belt to hold the customers in the bed, but that left great big tan lines across their stomachs. So now Kitty just has the thing standin' on its end. It's a chore to get it closed, but personally I think the results are much better. And if you ask real nice, some of them kids playin' the video games right next to you will help you close the two sections together. For $5 a session on Wednesday mornin's you can also use Kitty's weight room. Well, it really ain't a real weight-liftin' room, but more of a storage room, and instead of liftin' weights, you help unload the tires off the truck and lift them up onto the shelves. But regardless, you do get a good workout.

Kyle, Kitty's husband, is still pourin' drinks down at Anita's Bar and Grill. He loves his job, and Anita says he's real good at it.

Lot #12

Sister Bertha and her group of self-righteous hens have finally come up with a name for themselves. They are officially the Sin Stoppers. They rented out a buildin' from my niece, Lulu Bell, the simple land baron that she is, and fixed it all up so that it would be their official Sin Stoppers headquarters. I mean they spent tons of money makin' it look good inside. After all, that buildin' was about five years from bein' condemned by the state of Arkansas, which means it had about a year left

till it fell down on its own. But Lulu Bell didn't tell Sister Bertha that. She
might be slow, folks, but she ain't dumb. Anyways, two days before it
was scheduled to officially open, a twister came along and blew the
whole thing to pieces. Truly, when the dust had settled there wasn't nothin'
but the foundation left. There wasn't a sign of the new furniture or pam-
phlets or nothin' that them Sin Stoppers had put in that place. Luckily
for Lulu Bell, the whole place was covered by her insurance, but no one
in Sister Bertha's camp had even thought about gettin' some kind of
renters' insurance. It was a total loss for the SS (Sin Stoppers, that is).

In an attempt to recoup their losses, the SS decided to hold a great
big yard sale in Sister Bertha's yard. You should have seen it. These
ladies had brought stuff in by the truckload at six A.M. for the eight A.M.
published startin' time, and it took 'em right up to eight to get everything out. They had stuff stacked up all the way into the street right in
front of Sister Bertha's trailer. It looked like they were gonna do real
well. And then the clouds moved in at ten till eight. Within just a few
minutes it rained like I've never seen it rain, I'm talkin' torrential downpour. The roof of my trailer sounded like somebody was slammin' golf
balls down on it. And the flash flood, oh, it was terrible. It was so heavy,
you couldn't see more than four feet in front of you. And after almost an
hour of this unusual downpour, it just went away as fast as it had come.
The sun came out, and the birds started singin' again. And as we all as-
cended from our trailers we were amazed to feel the cool breeze that
softly made its way through the High Chaparral and that not one yard
sale item was left in Lot #12. It had all washed away and down about a
mile into the fields of the O'Connor brothers. Now, I need to tell you
that the O'Connor brothers and Sister Bertha don't get along. You see,
them boys and their families are Church of Christ, which in Sister Bertha's
book is just one step up from the Catholics. So when she's drivin' the
Holier Than Most Baptist Church Sunday school bus, she likes to get on
that intercom as she passes by their farms and yell, "If y'all will look over
to your left, y'all will see people who are goin' to hell." Pastor Ida May
Bee has told her many times to stop that kind of behavior, but her hands
are tied on account of Sister Bertha's power in the church. In any case,
when her and the Sin Stoppers tried to get the yard sale items that had
floated into the brothers' field, the boys started shootin' at 'em. Of
course those ladies took off runnin' for cover like a brood of chicks. There
was no reasonin' with them O'Connor boys neither. They knew they
had that evil old cow over a barrel and they weren't givin' in. Finally the

ladies just dispersed, and went on to their homes in defeat. The O'Connor brothers had an auction in their yard about a month later and took in close to $20,000. And since none of them SS woman read my books, I guess it's safe to say that me and Pastor Ida May Bee sneaked up there and made off with a few real good items. Did I mention that Pastor Ida May Bee and the O'Connor brothers get along real real good?

Lot #13

With Mickey Ray Kay doin' as well as he is at Lamb's Sodas, and his wife, Connie Kay, and his mother, Wanda Kay, both workin' at Connie's Merle Norman store, he thought it might be a good time to somehow share the blessin's they've gotten with others. So Mickey Ray and his wife and mother moved the weights out from his workout fitness room, which I don't think had been used for years, into the outside shed. Then the gals got to cleanin' and remodelin' until that little dingy cracker box of a room was just pure elegant. After all that, the Kays did somethin' that no one would have ever guessed they'd ever have done. They volunteered to take in one of them foreign exchange students. I guess the part that shocked us the most was that Mickey Ray and Connie had decided long ago not to not have kids so they could follow their careers in life, kind of like me and my husband, and now here they are, in their late thirties, openin' their trailer home up to a non-American youngster.

You'd have thought it was Christmas day when fifteen-year-old Brigitte Bucher arrived at Lot #13. She was about as beautiful as a gal that age could get with her pale skin, blue eyes, and long blond hair. She looked like an angel, although looks can be deceivin'. Accordin' to Connie, it was pure hell from the get-go. They couldn't do anything right in that girl's eyes. For example, on the very first mornin' after she'd arrived, Connie and Wanda fixed her up a real nice traditional breakfast, but all Brigitte did was look at the plate full of French toast and French fries, the glass of French wine, and the freshly opened pack of cigarettes that they'd placed in front of her. Then she looked up at them and shouted, "Êtes-vous les idiots?" and "*Essayez-vous de me tuer avec ces ordures?*" which I don't think means "thank you" in French. She then jumped up and ran out the door. The folks from the exchange student place came by that day and picked up Brigitte's suitcase and clothes. Poor Mickey Ray and Connie were just heartbroken and blamed themselves for the whole incident.

"Maybe if we'd given her French cigarettes the whole thing would've ended up different," Connie once told me as she tried to hide the tears, "but Kitty ain't got no French cigarettes for sale over at Gas and Smokes." Of course you have to buy somethin' from one of the many lines of products that she peddles door to door when she breaks down on you like that. I've tried to avoid the subject completely 'cause to be honest with y'all, I ain't got no more room in my bathroom for another bottle of Skin-so-soft.

Lot #14

If you haven't guessed by now, Dottie Lamb and Ben Beaver are couple number three in that big June 21 weddin'. Yes, they finally announced publicly the fact that all of us had guessed on our own that both these widowers were a serious couple. Y'all will recall if you read my first book that Dottie's husband died sometime back, and how in my holiday book I tell you about Ben's wife's passin'. Well, you should see that ring on Dottie Lamb's finger. That diamond, which you just know she got at a huge discount, could blind a child who stared directly at the light it casts. And happy, why Dottie is so happy she was almost able to form a smile in that Botox'd face of hers when we talked about her and Ben just last week. Now she assures me that Ben sleeps in one room and she sleeps in the other, and to that I assured her that I wore a size twelve. Of course Dottie and Ben both hope all the hoopla at her store (see Lot #16 for details) will all be over and done with before the weddin' in June. In any case, keep all three of these couples in your prayers, and hopefully I'll have weddin' photos in my next book, or even before that online. We will just have to wait and see.

Lot #15

You know, I just love Kenny and Donny. They are two of the funniest men I've ever known. Talk about your wit! Why, even some of the jokes or comments I don't get are still funny as all get-out. They're just two fellas who enjoy life to the fullest, which is why Donny floored me when he said he was gonna grow a full-length beard.

"Now why would you go off and do somethin' like that," I asked. Well, it seems that everywhere he goes, people are always mistakin' him for a woman, and I don't just mean in the drive-thru neither. Durin' a trip to Dallas, the boys went to that Sixth Floor Museum at Dealey Plaza where our beloved president was assassinated forty years ago. (By the way, if you go to *www.earthcam.com/jfk/* you can view a live Web cam from the alleged sniper's perch on the sixth floor inside the former Texas School Book Depository.) Inside they do a kind of check-in where you have to leave your camera bag and such, since photos ain't allowed up on the sixth floor. They've got lots of photos up there that are copyrighted and they don't want people snappin' copies of 'em. Well, Donny, who has a full mustache and hadn't even shaved his face that day, takes his camera bag strap off his shoulder and places it in front of the guard that is workin'. Donny smiles at him, and the guard smiles back.

"Are you wantin' to check your camera bag, madam?" the guard asks as he looks Donny dead in the face.

In the deepest voice he can muster, Donny replies, "I would like to check in my camera case if you don't mind."

To this the guard says, "Great," and then tears off half of a claim ticket and hands it to Donny. "Thank you, madam, and have a nice day," the guard says without missin' a beat.

Well, that was it. Donny was determined to grow a full Grizzly Adams beard. Of course neither his roommate, Kenny, or I actually know how long this whole beard thing will last. After all, Kenny says that if Donny does grow a beard, Donny won't be able to drink for free at any of the bars like he normally does on ladies' nights. We'll just have to see.

Lot #16

My husband, Dew's mother-in-law, Momma Ballzak, is doin' peachy keen. She still has her job arrangin' the plastic flowers at the Vance Pool Funeral Center as well as her part-time jobs, which include sellin' her used margarine, whippin' cream, and cottage-cheese–style containers (Trailer Park Tupperware, as she calls it) at in-home private parties and down at the flea market, and cleanin' rooms down at the R.U. Inn. As a matter of fact, Tina Faye has said that once she's added them one hundred rooms to the R.U. Inn, she'd like to have Momma Ballzak be the general manager over housekeepin'. Tina Faye told her that all she'd have to do is come in, check on the computer to see if the girls had cleaned the rooms, and if they hadn't, cuss 'em out from one end to the other, and then tell 'em to clean the rooms now. Momma Ballzak can do that, so she said she'd take the promotion. And in the meantime she's been workin' along with my Me-Ma part-time down at Lamb's Super Store, which is havin' lots of trouble itself with Sister Bertha's Sin Stoppers.

Accordin' to the SS and the signs that they carry just off the property, Lamb's Super Store is promotin' pornography inside the buildin' itself. Well, one thing Dottie Lamb ain't is a pornographer, and what it all boils down to is that Dottie and her dog-ugly daughter, Opal, decided to start carryin' women's undergarments like plain old-fashioned bras and what some call granny panties along with slips in their store. And in an attempt to promote these new goods and let shoppers know that they were sellin' 'em now, they hired women to walk around in these items throughout the store, answerin' any questions customers might have. It ain't like they were runnin' around in lingerie. And to be honest, you see a lot more flesh at any swimming pool nowadays. The whole thing was stupid, but Sister Bertha insists it is pornography plain and simple, even though she hasn't even seen the modelin' in person. So let me state right here and now to everybody out there includin' Sister Bertha, that my Me-Ma and Momma Ballzak ridin' around Lamb's Super Store on two of them mobility scooters at two miles an hour dressed in a white bra, granny panties, and a slip have never been and will never be anyone with half a brain's idea of pornography. I'm tellin' y'all that not even a Mennonite would be turned on by these two. So drop your idiotic cause, and, for cryin' out loud, let Momma Ballzak make some extra liquor money. After all, have you seen the way she looks? She could use a drink to kill the pain.

Lot #17

Tina Faye has had nothin' but good news in the past few months. It seems that just behind the motel that she owns, the R.U. Inn, which, as you know, is named after her daddy, they found oil in that land, and some big company has paid her a large amount of money just to have the rights to drill. Well, Tina Fay couldn't be happier as you might have guessed. Since this announcement, Tina has decided to add a meetin' hall and an additional one hundred rooms to the thirteen the motel already had. Of course, since the place is real big with seniors, Tina Faye has decided to buy more land and instead of buildin' upwards, which could cause a problem for her guests, she's just gonna build outwards. Of course this means that the ice machine is about a quarter of a mile from the last room.

Faye Faye LaRue, on the other hand, doesn't seem to be doin' so well in the business world. For some odd reason the Danglin' Tassel has been havin' problems drawin' folks in. It seems that the Blue Whale Strip Club is stealin' its thunder, if you can believe that. I don't know if it's 'cause of the good food they got or simply my sister's rise to fame with that bartendin' guide of hers. But in any case, before you feel sorry for Faye Faye, just remember that she's got a good business head on her shoulders. She still has a few new tricks up her sleeves. For example, she's just started puddin' wrestlin' a month and a half ago. Every night of the week with the exception of Sunday when they're closed, at about 8:00 P.M. they lay plastic tarps on the stage and then pull out a turtle pool full of banana puddin'. Then two of their bikini-clad dancers, or "old hags" as my sister, Donna Sue, calls 'em, kneel down in the pool and when the whistle is blown they wrestle. After the first match, the winner gets to take on any man in the audience who will pay $10 to get in the pool. Well, business has picked up a bit for Faye Faye, although from what I hear, the Tassel is startin' to smell like somebody put a loaf of banana bread in an old sneaker. I also hear that they're switchin' over to the sugar-free banana puddin' as well on account of what it's doin' to the dancer's skin and all. One tip for all you menfolk, if you're gonna wrestle, go on Monday nights. That's when the banana puddin's fresh.

And yes, Faye Faye is still workin' on that trailer park horoscope book of hers, so just be patient.

Lot #18

Now I ain't gonna air my dirty laundry out here in print. I'd rather do it on the Internet so everybody can see what me and my husband, Dew, have been up to. I will tell you what I have been workin' on though. As many of y'all know, I spend a lot of time on the road, and things happen to me that, well, let's just say I've never mentioned to y'all in my books before. I'm sure y'all are wonderin' what kinds of things I'm talkin' about, so I might as well tell you. Over the years I've had several murders take place around me. You'd have thought I'd be frightened out of my wits, but since I've seen practically every *Murder, She Wrote,* that just ain't the case. So I've finally decided to take pen to paper and try my hand at writin' down some of these events where I've managed to actually solve the crime. Now, I don't know if anyone will publish my mysteries, but what the heck, I just have this urge to share these stories with y'all any-ways. But I'll have more on that at a later time.

So go on over to *www.rubyannboxcar.com* and take a look at my Web page. Feel free to visit the links, which will take you to the official pages of the Blue Whale Strip Club, which, thank the Lord, ain't got no nudity on it, Lamb's Super Store, where you can buy items featurin' folks from the trailer park on 'em, and even Holier Than Most Baptist Church. So get online and stop by my place anytime.

Lot #19

Vance Pool has been busy as a beaver with his funeral home busi-ness. Now I don't mean that to sound as if people are droppin' like flies around here, but simply that he's been off out of town openin' up his line of new "Funeral Centers." He's got Harry and Elroy runnin' the local funeral home while he's away. It ain't the same around the trailer park without 400-pound Vance Pool around. You can actually go out of your trailer without fear of runnin' into him while he's wearin' nothin' but a Speedo. As anyone with even the slightest sight in one eye can imagine, that's a relief for all of us. Elroy is still sleepin' out in the shed with his dog, Zero, and Harry is takin' care of the trailer itself. But what they have done is take in a part-time roommate while Vance is gone out of town, with his permission of course. But just like anything else here in the High Chaparral Trailer Park, it turned out to be very controversial at first.

The new roommate was none other than Flora Delight, the stripper with the wooden leg whom some of y'all will recall from my sister's book, *Donna Sue's Down Home Trailer Park Bartending Guide*. Now, despite what Sister Bertha might have been sayin' at the time, Flora did not move into Lot #19 so she could engage in immoral behavior with the menfolk of the trailer park. She moved in there simply on account of the fact that her little shack she had in Searcy burnt to the ground, and she had no other place to stay. Chef Bernie and Melba Toast as well as my sister, Donna Sue, offered to put her up in a motel, but she re-fused 'cause she didn't want them to have to put out that kind of money. So when former male dancers Elroy and Harry heard about her dilemma, they called Vance, whom y'all will also recall is a former dancer himself, and asked if he'd mind if she slept in his bed while he was away. Bein' the good soul that he is, he agreed with the boys and told 'em to go ahead and ask her. Needless to say, she couldn't say no; after all, it would just be until she got a check from the insurance company, and then she could rebuild. You see, she lost everything she had on that dreadful night when fire tore through her little house. As a matter of fact, she was lucky to have escaped with her life. The fire was so bad that it swept through the house like it was made out of paper, forcin' her to quickly strap on her leg and flee, grabbin' what little she could on the way out the front door. Unbeknownst to Flora was the fact that her wood leg was actually spreadin' the fire as she went from room to room. It wasn't until she'd made it clear of the house that she realized she was on fire. Luckily, the dew in the wet grass put out her leg as she dropped and rolled. And with the exception of her blackened wooden appurtenance, Flora was fine. The good news was that most of her stuff was still in mini storage 'cause she hadn't had the money to pay on the back rent yet. And since she had renter's insurance on that shack she'd called home, it would only be a few months before she could collect. In the meantime she had no place to live, and she would have to take the stage each night at the Blue Whale Strip Club with that old burned leg. Flora says that just as soon as that insurance check arrives, she will be gettin' a place of her own. So keep her in your prayers.

Lot #20

Most of y'all will recall that Little Linda has moved into Lot #20 and called it home. Her daytime business, the Beauty Barge, is doin' pretty good. Y'all will recall that it's a floatin' beauty shop over on the lake, which most of us in the trailer park go to now that one of our own owns it. Of course she ain't a beautician or nothin' like that, but simply the gal with the deed and the keys, which she won durin' a poker game down at the Last Stop Nursing Home. You see, even though she's got a criminal record as long as both arms and still enough to go around one thigh, she's also got a kind heart for the elderly and animals. At least twice a month Little Linda volunteers down at the nursin' home as a sort of "candy stripper." Mind you, she don't strip, but she does wear semi-revealin' clothes, which the fellas down there seem to enjoy. But for the most part, she leads all the seniors in games like Simon says, charades, and crack the whip. And from time to time she even plays cards with 'em. Well, one night after a game of spades, this cigarette-smokin', foul-mouthed, rather rough old gal demanded a game of poker. Long story short, the gal was none other than Deloris Fink, owner of the then-named Fink's Floating Beauty Palace, and when the cards had all been played and all the chips counted, Little Linda left the buildin' that night with the keys and deed to what would soon be known as the Beauty Barge. She also came home that night with a set of dentures, a half-used tube of ointment, two bedpans, and a walker. Of course she exchanged the later items for her blouse, both shoes, and her bra. Did I forget to mention that they was playin' strip poker as well? Who says cataracts can't be a blessin'?

I told y'all in my last book that she'd got her old beat-up RV parked in the lot and was waitin' for the repo trailer that she bought from the bank to arrive just as soon as the people who owned it could be located and the trailer could actually be repossessed. Well, you should have seen her face light up when Sheriff Gentry stopped by to let her know that they finally found the trailer. It'd somehow managed to make it all the way over to a little teeny tiny town just south of Guadalajara, Mexico. Don't ask me how it got there, 'cause nobody knows, but accordin' to Sheriff Gentry, the police captain in Guadalajara told him that it was in excellent condition. The bad news was that it was gonna cost a lot more to ship it back to the High Chaparral Trailer Park than the trailer was actually worth. Needless to say, Little Linda was brokenhearted. So she instructed Sheriff Gentry to just tell the captain to go on ahead and sell the dang thing and then send the money to her. Well, about two weeks later an envelope arrived in the mail with a Mexican postmark on it. Not knowin' how to speak Spanish, Little Linda brought it over to me to look at. Of course I don't know how to speak Spanish either, but sometimes I can make out an occasional word, especially if it's food related. When she opened the envelope and read the check that was inside, she nearly passed out. Accordin' to her, she'd paid $5,000 for the trailer and the check was for $7,600. She was so excited. Well, I drove her down to the bank since she couldn't get her RV to start, shock surprise. I can tell you, that was one trip I wished I hadn't made. First there was all the yellin' from bein' excited and then once the bank told her that the check was made out in pesos and not dollars, makin' it worth a mere $733.47, there was all the cryin' and emotional outbursts on the way back.

If the trailer thing wasn't bad enough, you should have met her last boyfriend. That man couldn't have won a mental challenge with a can of nuts. Lord, he was stupid! Of course that explains why he did what he did. One mornin' shortly after the whole Mexican trailer debacle, Little Linda and him decided to take a trip into town. Seein' how he didn't have a car and hers still wasn't workin', they tried to start up the RV. Well, even after this fella had unhooked the electric line from the RV, and tried to start up the vehicle, he could still get the radio and all, but it wouldn't crank up. So, bein' the smart thing that he was, he decided to crawl under the RV to look at the engine. Sure enough, he got under there and messed around a bit with some tools, when all of a sudden it started up. It also started to move as well. The fool had left the car in drive and now he was under it. Well, he started yellin' an' screamin' like a little girl. Little Linda heard his cries for help as they passed underneath her, but since she was in the bathroom at the time, there was nothin' she could do but hang on for the ride. He boyfriend managed to get out in the nick of time and just as the sewage line was ripped from the RV. Instead of chasin' after it and tryin' to get back inside, the idiot just picked up rocks and threw it at the slowly movin' vehicle in an attempt to stop it. As luck would have it, Kyle Chitwood, who was puttin' a bag of trash into the dumpster by the gate, saw the RV movin' and heard the screams. Bein' the quick-thinkin' man that he is, he ran to the door and managed to get it open, but just as he started to jump in, he was hit in the head by a rock, and he fell to the ground. Bein' the cowboy that he also is, he jumped back up to his feet and climbed inside the RV as it crossed the road and smashed through the bushes between Lot #13 and Lot #16. Kyle slammed on the breaks, stoppin' the RV just inches from his very own trailer parked in Lot #11. As luck would have it, the only thing hurt that day were a few bushes and the RV's bathroom door, which was knocked off its hinges when the halfway-clothed Little Linda came flyin' out from the sudden stop. As you can guess, she dumped that boyfriend that same day. The menfolk helped her get her RV back over to her lot since it wouldn't start back up, Ben Beaver ordered her a new sewage line, and she's put up a blanket on the bathroom doorway. Last I heard, the cost to replace and install the sewage line as well as repair the door and replace the bushes should cost Little Linda right around $735. God bless her, she can't win for losin'.

Chapter 1

Family

Lulu Bell of Lot #8 goes trick-or-treatin' with her daddy.

*f*olks, let me tell you, there ain't no way that y'all would ever believe the huge amount of cards, letters, and e-mails I get from folks all around the world who are in critical need of advice about handlin' their loved ones. For some unknown reason y'all just can't cope with your people. I'm tellin' you, y'all get along better with your neighbors than you do with them folks you call family. I mean, sure, I got problems with my kin. After all, I'm just like anybody else. Why, who wouldn't with a sister and a mother in-law who are usually so tanked on any given day that you could set off firecrackers in the holes of their jelly shoes and they'd think they was gettin' a foot massage. I got a thirty-five-year-old niece that's so Looney Toons that this past Halloween she put her daddy's ashes, which she still carries with her at all times, in a empty Count Chocula cereal box with a paper sack Scotch-taped to the front of it just so he could go trick or treat with her. My Me-Ma is so far gone that for Christmas in honor of the gift of "God givin' us Jesus," she gave us all homemade lip balm, which she'd personally created by combinin' Crisco, car wax, and grape jelly and then puttin' it in creatively decorated empty film canisters. Thanks to that crazy old lady, my dear mentally challenged niece's fiancé, Billy Bob, was sick for two weeks and almost saw Jesus face-to-face. And as far as my momma and daddy go, well, don't even get me started. And my husband is so enthralled with the world of fishin' that I got to open a can of tuna and dab on little of that spring fresh water behind my ears just to get his attention. But let me tell y'all, I'm not bitter. No, unlike the folks who take pen to paper askin' for my divine wisdom, I'm able to find the faults in my kinfolk,

35

point 'em out, and get over 'em. I'm not one to carry a grudge or let a predicament fester like y'all do. As a matter of fact, everyone in my family simply deals with a problem head-on, and then we just let it go, which is why this past January we signed Me-Ma up for them month-long daily experimental high-colonic treatments at the Last Stop Nursing Home where she lives. I got a feelin' that this year when we all join together in love and joy to celebrate our Savior's birth, the gifts from the old lady will be a little better and less dangerous. In any case, I do hope that the followin' letters as well as my thought-out responses will help you to find a way to deal with the people that make up your clan. And remember that regardless of what happens, you're stuck with 'em, so make the best out of it.

And now, on to your letters.

The Mister and the Missus

Dear Ruby Ann,

Is there any correct answer to the question "Do these jeans make my butt look big?" I can tell you that "No, your butt makes those jeans look big" is not acceptable.

—Frightened

Dear Frightened,

This is a real tough one, especially if you're religious. The last thing you want to do is lie to the one you love, but you also don't want to commit a sin. Of course if you happen to be one of them "Once Saved Always Saved Baptists" then you got no problem at all. But all us regular Baptists and the rest of the world are still stuck with a dilemma. Here is what I'd do if I was you and that question happened to come up again. First off I'd answer back with a question like "Are you kiddin'?" or "Are you serious?" or "Are you talkin' to me?"

Then when she replies back with a yes, simply reply back with "My dear, you are just as sexy and as hot as you were when I first fell in love with you." Then give her a big old kiss and quickly leave the room. If that don't work, I'd suggest you take her out on a shoppin' spree and push the dresses or skirts so you never have to answer that question again.

> Love, Kisses, and Trailer Park Wishes,
> Ruby Ann Boxcar

Hi, Ruby Ann,

I bought my husband a Tracker boat—the Silver Anniversary Edition—for Christmas 2002. This was going to benefit my husband by getting him to go fishing every weekend and benefit myself by him going fishing. Now that the weather is nice, my husband wants me to go fishing with him every weekend. How do I tell him that that was not the reason I bought him the boat?

> Best Regards,
> D.K. Pierce

Dear D.K.,

Goodness sakes, no! Don't tell him nothin'. Just smile and say you'd love to go fishin' with him. I know this is the last thing you want to do, but trust me on this, go—but follow my advice to the letter. By the way, I'm assumin' that you got him the V-18 model? My husband, Dew, has one of those, and, boy, does he love it. Anyways, gettin' back to your letter, the first thing you want to do is bring along stuff that you won't need. An example of this would be a portable battery-operated TV set or a tape player and one of those books on tape that you can rent from the library. Try to get a love story tape if you can find one. Then while y'all are out on the water, turn on a soap opera or pop in that tape and play it loud enough for him to hear it as well. The next thing you will want to do is have him bait your hook and cast your line. Tell him that you don't like that portion of the lake where he has you, and would he please try again, a little farther and to the left. When he has recast you, quickly come back with "Well, you almost got it where I wanted it." See if he will do it again. If not, thank him for "at least tryin' to get it in the right place" and give him a little kiss. Follow this up with "I'm sure you did your best anyways." Then just set back and listen to the TV or book on tape. If you brought a sack lunch, take your sandwich out and eat it quickly. Then ask him if he would like one as well. When he says yes, pull it out of the sack, and as you try and hand it to him, do your best to rock the boat a bit and toss it in the lake. Tell him you are sorry, but it slipped right out of your hand. Tell him you will just gently toss the bag over to him, and do so. When he opens the bag and sees that the only things left inside are a few prunes and a diet bar, tell him you feel so bad for droppin' his sandwich, and maybe next time you should just stay at home. You can repeat that line about stayin' at home next time once again on your way home, after you've accidentally knocked the bait container overboard and dropped your fishin' pole in the water as well. The next time he decides to go fishin', he might ask you, but if you simply say that you've got stuff to do around the house, but you hope he has a good time, he won't argue with you.

> Love, Kisses, and Trailer Park Wishes,
> Ruby Ann Boxcar

Dear Ruby Ann,

My husband of seven years just doesn't listen to me anymore. He acts as if he couldn't care less about what I have to say to him. Sometimes he really hurts my feelings and I want him to know that. What can I do?

> Kim

Dear Kim,

Boy, hon, don't I know how you feel. When it comes to my husband, Dew, there are times that I think he don't even know that I'm alive. Don't get me wrong, my husband, Dew, is a good man, and still quite the catch, but there are times that I swear if I didn't bite my nails down to stubs, I'd scratch his eyes out. Well, I guess it ain't really that bad. But on any given Saturday or Sunday when one of his fishin' shows is on boob tube, there ain't nothin' goin' on but him and that dang big-screen TV. I've even stripped down to nothin' but my glasses and a handful of hairpins and rolled around and jumped up and down all around the livin' room of our two story double-wide tryin' to get that man's attention, and all I got for my seductive actions was some bad carpet burns and two flat tires on the front of the trailer home. Well, Kim, I finally waited until my husband was in one of his playful moods, if you know what I mean. That was when I knew I had his undivided attention. I told him that before we blacked out the bedroom windows with foil, turned all the lights off, stuffed towels in cracks of the door to keep out the light, and put on that *Chipmunks Sing Barry White's Greatest Hits* album, I had a few things to say. Of course he gave me one of those "do I have to" looks and all, but that man was all ears. Not wantin' to spoil the moment, I kept it short and sweet and told him that from time to time there are certain things a woman like me needs to hear. I told him that if he wanted to make me happy, then all he'd need to do was occasionally say, "I'm sorry," "I love you," "Have you lost weight?" "I like your family," "No dear, it's not burnt, it's just well done," "You look nice," "That smell is natural," "They look very firm," "Thanks for cookin'," "I'm sure that chair was cracked before you sat in it," or "Regardless of what anybody says, your feet look great in sandals." Needless to say, before that episode of *Baywatch* that he was viewin' at the time was over, he'd promised that he would be more carin'. And needless to say, bein' the good man that he is, my husband, Dew, has kept his word. Of course I still ain't been able to break him of that habit he has of tellin' me to get my "great big frozen sasquatch feet" off him when we go to bed at night. But I can live with that, after all, at least he knows I'm there.

Love, Kisses, and Trailer Park Wishes,
Ruby Ann Boxcar

Dear Ruby Ann,

I am writing you in order to get your help to save my marriage of ten years, because my wife is out of control. She has become an eBay junkie—she bids on all kinds of stuff that we don't need or will ever need. In the past three months she has bought three wedding dresses, and, like I said, we have been married for ten years already. She also has been bidding on Civil War memorabilia and she is from New Jersey. She buys underwear by the case and not even in her size. She sits at the computer all day and sometimes she never gets out of her bathrobe, not to mention the times when she doesn't even shower. I am holding down two jobs and I still can't get ahead of the bills that are coming in. We are going to be evicted if things don't improve, so I am begging you. Help!

Signed,
Held Hostage in Cyberspace

Dear Held Hostage,

Most folks would tell you to just cut up them credit cards or close your wife's checkin' account, but not me. You see, me and my husband went through the same thing a while back with his momma. Now, I love my mother in-law to death, but sometimes she gets drunk and just spends hours on that computer buyin' anything she can find. Even though me and my husband, Dew, try and stay out of Momma Ballzak's life, and let her live it as best she sees fit, when the deep-sea-fishin' gear arrived at her Arkansas trailer, we stepped in. Of course seein' how she's a grown woman it wasn't like we could tell her no more Internet surfin', and even if we had, we couldn't be there to watch over her all the time in order to make sure she followed our guidelines. So we went with plan B.

One night my husband went out to her electric box out back behind her trailer and turned off the switch. Normally we wouldn't mess with anythin' electric, but since the kids in the surroundin' area as well as several of her old vengeful boyfriends do the same thing to my sister's trailer on a weekly basis, we knew it was safe. Well, when Momma Ballzak called over on her cell phone that we done gave her last year after that terrible funeral parlor incident (see *Ruby Ann's Down Home Trailer Park Guide to Livin' Real Good* for the whole story on that event) to tell us that her "electric had done dried up," my husband went over and turned it back on. He then told his momma that he'd need to check out her computer to make sure that it wasn't severely damaged by the outage. Well, what he did was he disconnected her DSL and installed an internal modem that he'd picked up for pennies at the local thrift store. He told her that the phone lines on her trailer lot were damaged and would never be able to connect as fast as they had before. Of course she was disappointed, but she was still happy to be able to get online. Mind you, she still tries to buy everything she finds on eBay or them other online stores, but with a 14.4 connection, she typically ain't the highest bidder any longer. We've noticed that she's also comin' out of the trailer a little more often here lately as well as cleanin' herself up. I could be wrong, but I think she's gettin' tired of the whole thing. Especially since by the time her bid actually registers now with that new connection, the auction is over.

Love, Kisses, and Trailer Park Wishes,
Ruby Ann Boxcar

Dear Ruby Ann

I thought married people were supposed to be open and honest with each other, but my new hubby blabbed secrets I shared from work and now I'm in deep spit! HELP.

Puzzled Bride

Dear Puzzled Bride,

Married folks are supposed to be open and honest with one another, and I'm sure y'all were, but, well, I don't care how hot your husband might be, or even if he likes his adult beverages shaken and not stirred, unless he's got three digits after his last name, don't expect him to keep any kind of secrets. And I do mean any kind of secrets, if you catch my drift. Of course, there is a way to shut him up, but it can occasionally backfire if not used correctly. What you do is wait until he makes some kind of goof or blunder, and it don't matter in which room of the house or trailer he makes it. Then when you've got a few friends over for dinner, simply tell the story. Not only will this get your husband redder than a tomato, it will also let him know just how you felt when he told your secrets around town. The only thing is that you want to make sure you do this in front of just a few close personal friends. Otherwise he just might not forgive you. And more than likely, he's gonna ask you why you had to tell that story or why you brought it up, or even how he thought that was just between you and him. Simply tell him that since he told your secrets you thought it would be all right to share his as well. Then add this line, "But if you'd rather that we keep these kinds of things to ourselves, then that would be fine as well." Now I've got to warn y'all that this is gonna feel pretty good, especially since this is most likely the first time you've ever had the pleasure of manipulatin' your new husband. Well, dear newlywed, enjoy the high, 'cause as time goes by, you're gonna be doin' a whole lot more of it, I can tell you that. Anyways, this little talk the two of you have should take care of the openness-and-honesty issue without worryin' about what your husband will reveal in the future. I know that bein' the little innocent newly married gal that you are, you don't understand why you just can't come out and say, "Hey, don't tell people the stuff that I tell you in private," but trust me and millions of wives around the world when I say, that stuff don't work. So just follow my advice, and you and your man will be just fine. Good luck!

> Love, Kisses, and Trailer Park Wishes,
> Ruby Ann Boxcar

Dear Ruby Ann,

What is the best way to convince my husband to take the dishes out of the sink before he pees in it? PLEASE HELP!

> Signed
> Peeved at Peed-on Dishes

Dear Peeved,

I don't know how old you are, but trust me, hon, when I say that men are like beets, there's only so much you can do with 'em. Especially when it comes to menfolk, old habits die hard, but I do have a suggestion other than puttin' a toaster in the sink and pluggin' it in. I suggest that you simply pack away the good dishes till you get an electric dishwasher and in the meantime, switch to paper plates.

> Love, Kisses, and Trailer Park Wishes,
> Ruby Ann Boxcar

Dear Ruby Ann,

Who should cook dinner? And should the person who doesn't cook dinner, especially if he's unemployed and doesn't have anything better to do all day while his wife is out earning minimum wage at the

Wal-Mart, have the right to whine about getting grilled cheese sandwiches and tomato soup for the fifth night in a row?

Signed,
All Tuckered Out

Dear Tuckered,

I actually need more information before handin' out specific wisdom. For example, is this husband of yours keepin' the home clean
and takin' care of the children? If so, then the answer is neither of
you should have to cook the dinner on a regular basis since y'all are
both workin' in your own ways. If that's the case, I'd say y'all should
grab a calendar and mark it up to where you and he cook every other
day. And if this ain't the case, then it would be nice to come home
from work to find a meal on the table even if it's delivered pizza or
Chinese. But I got to tell you that I personally would say you're as lazy
as that lay-around husband of yours. There you are, workin' at Wal-
Mart and you can't even find the time to grab some of that mighty
tasty food y'all got over in the concession stand before walkin' out the
door to head home. Shame on you as well. Remember, a relationship
is give and take, so you need to take home a good old-fashioned Wal-
Mart meal to give to that man of yours from time to time.

Love, Kisses, and Trailer Park Wishes,
Ruby Ann Boxcar

Dear Ruby Ann,

My husband is so lazy and inconsiderate. Here I'm busy with supper and the baby, and he's rattling his ice cubes at me, the signal I
should drop everything and refill his glass. Now our eight-year-old is
copying Daddy, so I've got man and boy to wait on. What should I do?

Tired of Hearing Ice Cubes Rattle

Dear Rattlin' Ice,

What should you do? It's more like what should you have done at
least eight years ago. You mean to tell me you've let this go on for

this long before complainin'? It was fine until now? Sister, from the way it sounds, if you could get money for stupidness, you'd be livin' high on the hog!

Luckily my husband, Dew, knows better than to act that way with me, but if he did, I'd simply start shakin' my glass when we are watchin' TV and tell him to get me somethin' to drink. If he said somethin', I'd tell him if he can't get up and get me a drink from time to time, then he needn't ever ask me to do the same for him. Or you could just simply get up, walk to the fridge, grab a can of whatever he's drinkin', throw it right at him, and yell, "Heads up!" If he asks why you did that, just say that you were on your way to the bathroom and could only stop for a second. If he complains about it, then tell him to get his own. If he keeps it up, then you keep throwin' 'em and headin' to the bathroom.

As far as the little one goes, be a parent and tell him to get his own and one for you and his daddy while he's at it.

Love, Kisses, and Trailer Park Wishes,
Ruby Ann Boxcar

Dear Ruby Ann,

I am seeking your advice because I know you have been around so much. I have been through many relationships in my life. I now have been settled for over ten years and am happy, but we are finding it hard to keep the spark alive. We have tried all of the usual advice. You know—role-playing, games, and surprising each other at work or in the car and stuff. Nothing seems to work, and recently I have thought about bringing new life by stepping out. I have a feeling the apple of my eye already has, and seems all the happier for it, and except when I ask, it is not a subject for conversation. So what should I do? Just do it myself and not talk about it, cause a scene and try to get all the information, or just not sweat it at all?

Helpless

Dear Helpless,

Lots of folks write me about this same issue, and I have to tell you, it can be hard to find that same spark that brung you both together in a relationship that has been around for a while. Personally I think a lot of it has to do with all the day-to-day problems you have in your lives like bills, work, kids, mother-in-laws, and such. All that can dump a cold bucket of water on that flame of yours. And another problem is that y'all take each other for granted by now as well. Here is what I suggest doin'. One night get yourself an old shoe box and put it and all the family pictures on the dinner table. Both of you go through the photos with the idea that you are gonna put together a time capsule that will show what your relationship was like to either your kids or your grandkids or whoever. Find the early photos and both of you discuss what you saw in each other when you first met or on those first dates or even durin' that first year. Write that stuff down on a piece of paper. Put down the happy times as well as the not-so-happy times. Do that for each picture, and do about ten to twenty pics per each year that y'all have been together. More than likely, if that old spark is still there somewhere, it's gonna rekindle before the night is over. Y'all will fall in love with one another again, just like you did the first time. You will see the magic come back to life, the joy return, and the carin' spring anew. Of course, you might also find that your wick has burnt out, your magic trick is over, and somebody has dammed up the well.

But if you've rekindled that relationship again, then I got to tell you that I don't see nothin' wrong with "stepping out" like you mentioned. It does a body good to get out of the trailer or house once in a while, so why not? And you two should step out together once in a while. Don't just let him be the one, get in there and join him. I think y'all will both have a nice time together on the town enjoyin' a good meal or a fun movie or whatever else might sound entertainin'.

Love, Kisses, and Trailer Park Wishes,
Ruby Ann Boxcar

Momma and Daddy

Dear Ruby Ann,

I am really embarrassed, and you are the only one I can turn to since you are always so discreet. Since I'm an only son, my father has come to me with his problem, and to be honest, I wish I'd been born a girl so I never would have had to hear this story pass his lips. According to my sixty-year-old father, he hasn't been able to perform his manly commitments to my mother lately. I told him about how there are drugs that can help some people, but he wants to keep this whole thing private. Please help me, Ruby Ann. My relationship with my father has already been a bit tainted with his cry out for help. I'd like to just get this over with as soon as possible.

Yours truly,
Duke

Dear Duke,

I just might be the answer to your prayers. I know that Connie Kay told all us gals at an Avon party that her man, Mickey Ray Kay, had recently gone through the same experience that your daddy is havin'. Well, if you knew Mickey Ray, then you'd know that the last thing he'd ever do is talk to a doctor about his lack of manliness. And with his mother livin' in the trailer with 'em, it wasn't like they could actually try anythin' wild. But accordin' to Connie Kay, it all went north after she and Mickey Ray had finished watchin' an episode of that Anna Nicole show. Mickey Ray told Connie that after thirty minutes of that gal Connie looks like a great catch. So long story short, you might want get your daddy a *TV Guide* and have him turn on that Anna Nicole gal.

Love, Kisses, and Trailer Park Wishes,
Ruby Ann Boxcar

Dear Ruby Ann,

My sixty-seven-year-old mother is driving me to drink. She recently divorced Daddy and moved into my trailer. Now, I love her to death and all, but she's keeping me up night after night with all her howling and prowling. Granted, she's got her own bedroom, but as you may know, some trailers (mine to be precise) don't have real thick walls, so the sound comes right on through.

I've tried to talk to her about all the noise she's making and how she's got to keep it down as I have to go to work every morning at the Wal-Mart. But she won't hear of it. She just keeps telling me how she married Daddy when she was fifteen, and she's got plenty of oats to sow. And she's sowing them in the bedroom next to mine! And these oats don't have anything to do with farming, unless you're talkin' about the farmer himself. If you get my meaning. And this morning I saw my old third-grade teacher sneaking out the door at 6:00 A.M.—yuck! The tongues are waggin' in our trailer park. What am I to do?

Signed,
Daughter of a Born-Again Hussy

Dear DBAH,

I have a quick question for you. What in the heck were you doing up at 6:00 A.M. in a trailer park? No wonder the tongues are waggin'! I can assure you that nobody at the High Chaparral Trailer Park where I live would be seen awake at that time of day. Even when my husband, Dew, or some of the other menfolk in the trailer park get up early to go fishin', it ain't until at least 8:00 A.M. Why, even when I was a little girl and had to catch the bus to school, Momma and Daddy would set their alarm to go off no more than ten minutes earlier than the bus's normal arrival time. I was dressed and headin' out of the trailer at 8:47 with my schoolday breakfast, a Twinkie, shoved in my mouth, to catch the 8:48 A.M. bus each weekday mornin' for twelve years. So you can understand my questionin' about you bein' up an around at 6:00 in the mornin'. If you'd have been in bed where you belonged you never would have seen that old teacher of yours.

As for your momma, you should be glad that she don't just want to waste away in some old rockin' chair. It sounds like the problem is yours and not hers. I'd suggest you go out and get one of them sound machines, you know the kind that make sounds like waves or birds or trains and such. Turn that on when you go to bed and your dilemma will be solved. Sure y'all may still hear her moans, but with that sound machine you can pretend she's makin' them noises while tryin' to swim in the ocean or climbin' a mountain or runnin' alongside a steam engine. In any case, you just worry about who is sleepin' in your bed, and tell your momma to let the good times roll.

Love, Kisses, and Trailer Park Wishes,
Ruby Ann Boxcar

Dear Ruby Ann,

Well, it finally happened. After dating for over nine years, Rufus got around to proposing. Now that we're getting hitched, my mother wants to cook up a dinner party for us, which poses two problems. The first is that my mother is a gut-wrenching cook! The second is that her trailer only fits about eight people, and that's with everyone standing, and we have a whole passel of friends.

I've suggested a night out at the bowling alley (Rufus is one sexy bowler!), but she won't hear of it. She insists on cooking. Rufus and I don't want to hurt Momma's feelings, but the last time we ate her cooking we both spent the night fighting over the bathroom. I don't think our engagement or our bowels can take another episode like the last one.

What should we do?

Best,
Orlene

Dear Orlene,

Let me be the first to congratulate you on this joyous occasion, and I say this, of course, under the assumption that Rufus is a wonderful, carin' sort of fella. If he ain't, then let me be the first to tell you that maybe you should really give this whole marriage thing a second thought.

Movin' on, I totally understand where you're comin' from. After all, I have mistakenly eaten some of my Me-Ma's cookin'. She used to be able to cook up a storm, but as time has marched on her cookin' abilities have left with it. But in any case, I'd suggest that you and your man thank your momma for makin' the meal. Let her know how much it means to you. Then call up the bowlin' alley and reserve whatever you need for the gatherin'. I know this ain't makin' no kind of sense yet, but just trust me, 'cause I'm gettin' there.

On the mornin' of the get-together, go over to your momma's house, and call the electric company. Tell them you are her and you ain't payin' another dime on any future bills till they can lower the cost. Then demand that they get out there and shut your electricity off today. Just be rude, and keep sayin' that you won't pay. As you can guess, your momma ain't gonna have power to finish cookin' anythin', and whatever she already has cooked is gonna go bad in the fridge. So when she tells you that she has to cancel the dinner on account of some stupid idiot at the electric company, you can tell her that you understand, and that you will see if y'all can't pull some strings to get the bowlin' alley. Of course, as long as that woman is alive and breathin' air, you never tell this story to anyone. Do you got me? She ain't never got to know what you did. And don't feel bad if the electric company thinks she's some kind of quack. As long as she pays her bills on time, she won't have no kind of trouble with 'em. Of course she may have to take out a loan to cover the deposit they're gonna want in order to turn her electricity back on.

Love, Kisses, and Trailer Park Wishes,
Ruby Ann Boxcar

Dear Auntie Ruby Ann,

I hope I can call you Auntie because you feel like an aunt to me. HELP! My family is driving me crazy! A year and a half ago, they asked me to move back to Oklahoma City to help out with the family business and my father, who had suffered a seizure and mild aneurysm a few months prior. After a year and a half now, he's almost back to normal, except for the fact that he's even more of an old curmudgeon than ever. So, I gave up my prestigious Miami job and my apartment on SoBe to move back to fulfill my family duty. However, now that I've been back for a while, I find myself slowly losing my mind not only because of my insane family but because I've found myself completely urbanized after living in Dallas and Miami.

I do enjoy many aspects of country livin' (e.g., my house with the large garden/yard, friendly country folk, minimal gridlock, and short commute times, etc.) but find myself feeling alienated not only by my hillbilly family but by the culture shock of being back in OKC. I'd love to move to L.A. or even back to Miami or Dallas but feel like I'd be deserting my family, the family business, and my garden that I love. Not to mention that I'm getting too old to be moving all the time.

This dilemma has been slowly getting worse and weighing more heavily on my shoulders as time goes on. On the one hand, I love my family and am doing well for myself here in OKC. But on the other hand, my hillbilly family living in a hillbilly town is more than my poor, sensitive tastes can stand! I thought since you live in the High Chaparral Trailer Park and have a crazy family yourself, you might have some sage advice on how to keep my sanity—short of moving or turning to Prozac, intensive therapy, alcohol, etc. I'm already trying that!

Love,
Torn in a Twisted Family

Dear Torn,

As long as you keep buyin' my books, you can call me anythin' you want. With that said, let's clear a few things up right off the bat. Oklahoma City ain't a hillbilly town. I know many fine folks call it home, and I'm sure they'd be all up in arms to hear their fair city called "hillbilly." Sure, they might only have two or three nonacademic theaters, and only a handful of art galleries, which, compared to Miami or Dallas, ain't a whole lot, but that don't make it a hillbilly town. After all, they do get wrestlin' events and even had the American Idol tour come there last year.

When it comes to wacky families, I think mine takes the cake. And you're right, it can drive you nuts. However, your problem ain't with your family, but rather with you. You remind me of the gal who was stopped at an intersection complainin' about how bad the potholes were up ahead. "Fine," the driver behind her told her, "then just turn and go down a block rather than just settin' in the middle of the dang street." It sounds like all you can do is complain about the problem, which is easier for you than actually doin' somethin' about it. For example, if spendin' lots of time with your loved ones makes you crazy, then limit your time with 'em. And if you're livin' under the same roof, then get out of there and get your own place. Just remember that you came back home to help with your father and to help with the family business. Well, it sounds like your pa is fine, and your family business can do without you now. So either move or shut up. It's that simple. You did your part, so get out of there. Now if I'm wrong, and the family business still needs you for the time bein', then stay, but in order to keep your sanity, travel. That's what I do. I make sure that I'm away from the High Chaparral at least once every two months. You can drive to Dallas in less than four hours time even if you go the speed limit and count on traffic. And if that's too much, you can head up to Tulsa for a weekend and enjoy their culture. Sure, it still ain't Dallas, but it's a change from what you got now. So stop complainin' and do somethin'.

Love, Kisses, and Trailer Park Wishes,
Auntie Ruby Ann Boxcar

Dear Ruby Ann,

My momma used the gift certificate I gave her for her birthday to get the most butt-ugly tattoo I've ever seen. Now, not that it's in an area that a lot of people will ever see, but she wants my honest opinion of this "work of art." Do I lie and tell her it's the best money I ever spent or do I buy her another certificate for Christmas to have it removed?

Signed,
Love My Momma

Dear Momma Lover,

Have you ever been to a mall, to Wal-Mart, or even to Kmart, and seen them gals who can easily tip the scales at 200 pounds walkin' around in white stirrup polyester slacks stretched out so far that the good Lord himself couldn't even tell you what kind of material it's made out of? What I'm tryin' to say is that taste is in the eye of the beholder, which means your momma looks at that new tattoo in the same way them gals look at themselves in the mirror. In both cases, they are lovin' what they see. Who cares if it scares everybody else into fits of horror? And since it's where most people won't see it, then you got nothin' to worry about. So instead of givin' her negative feedback when she asks for your opinion on it, just simply tell her it looks great. After all, it is her private part and not yours that has to live with it for the rest of her life. So basically just shut the heck up and let her have fun.

Love, Kisses, and Trailer Park Wishes,
Ruby Ann Boxcar

Dear Ruby Ann,

When I talk to my parents (which is almost always a mistake) about getting a simple tongue stud or a nipple ring, they always say, "The Lord gave you seven holes in your body and that's enough." What can I say to that?

                                                    Pin Cushion Wannabe

Dear Wannabe,

Why don't you start off by tellin' 'em that y'all are some kind of sideshow freaks? Seven holes? Okay, let's take a count. You got two eye sockets or holes, two ear holes, two nasal holes, one mouth hole, and as we move on down the body, we got one hole in back and regardless of your sex, one in front. So that is two, four, six, seven, eight, nine holes that the normal person has in their body. You need to tell your folks that everybody else has nine holes, so you are deservin' of two more. Or you could simply wait until you move out of your parents' home and then get the extra holes added to your body.

Personally, I don't care for all that piercin' stuff simply 'cause it reminds me of one of my sister's old boyfriends that she dated back in 1972. He used to come to the dinner table with his shirt off and use his nipple rings as a napkin holder. Lord it was disgustin' to try and dine with him settin' there with a napkin danglin' out of one ring, and his readin' glasses hangin' from the other. At Christmas he'd decorate 'em with ornaments. He did show up not too long back and spent the night at her trailer. The next day he mowed what little grass she still had in her yard. The only thing was that it took him almost an hour to mow no more than a one-hundred-square-foot yard. God bless him, he kept gettin' his nipple rings caught in the lawn mower tires.

                          Love, Kisses, and Trailer Park Wishes,
                          Ruby Ann Boxcar

In-laws

Dear Ruby Ann,

I've been married to a wonderful man for sixteen years. The only problem we have is his mother. Although he is forty-two years old, she still treats him like a baby and tells him what to do. He hardly ever listens to me and when it comes to makin' an important decision he always calls her to ask her what she thinks. When we bought our trailer, she picked it out and went to the dealer to negotiate the deal. When we bought our new car ten years ago, she had to be the one that wheeled and dealed with the dealer. I just don't know what to do anymore. Even though our seventeen-year-old daughter and her boyfriend are livin' here until the baby is born, she wants us to convert the den into a room so she can live with us. Ruby, you're my only hope, please tell me how to get this situation under control.

> Love your books,
> Willa Mae

Dear Willa Mae,

This is simple. Invite the old lady over for a glass of milk or cup of coffee and a piece of pie. Then when she cuts into that pie, pull out the biggest dang gun you can buy and clean it at the table right in front of her. As you slowly put the bullets back in to it, simply explain that you think it's time for her to move on and enjoy her life without havin' to worry about you and your husband. "After all," you say lookin' directly at the gun, "life can be so short, don't you know?" Then look her straight in the eye and, after a beat, smile. This should do the trick. If not, then if the gun accidentally discharges, hittin' her handbag and flingin' it across the trailer, well, you can't be blamed for that.

> Love, Kisses, and Trailer Park Wishes,
> Ruby Ann Boxcar

Dear Ruby Ann,

I just got an invitation to a "Re-stocking" shower, hosted by my mother-in-law (it's a potluck, and the invitees have to bring food to share), for my recently divorced brother-in-law.

My mother-in-law is sending invitations to everyone she knows to solicit gifts to "re-stock" his now divorced household. Granted, he has four kids to care for when his ex-wife doesn't have them, but throwing a party and asking for gifts seems rude. My mother-in-law has even included a list of items that he needs like luggage! What do I do? Should I support this "shower" as she insists on calling it?

I always thought showers were a way to celebrate wonderful occasions like a marriage, or a baby, not a method for snagging a free item off a friend or family member. What do you think?

Kaylee Ann Justice

Dear Kaylee,

Maybe we should take a minute to look at showers or reasons to "celebrate wonderful occasions." Let's start off with baby showers. Just because two folks happened to forget to use or were just too lazy to get up out of bed or off the kitchen table and to grab some form of protection, I got to go out and spend my hard-earned money? Trust me, after thirteen years of marriage to the same man, somebody ought to throw me a doggone party when he can stay awake for more than two minutes after the lights have gone off at night. That deserves a gift! And a weddin' shower is even stupider if you ask me, 'cause in this case you got to spend more of your money just 'cause two people decided to get hitched. If you want a buy a gift for somebody, buy it for that married couple that lives next to you when they can go just one night without arguin' or screamin' to high heaven while you're tryin' to watch your favorite TV shows. That deserves a gift. So put your nose back in place and support this shower for your brother in-law. After all, it could be worse. He could be comin' over to your place askin' to borrow your luggage and such.

Love, Kisses, and Trailer Park Wishes,
Ruby Ann Boxcar

Dear Ruby Ann,

My mother-in-law caught me whisking crumbs off the table and onto the floor and says I'm a slut. Because of the baby crawling around, I mop the floor once a month whether it needs it or not.

Should I stuff the mop in mom's mouth or what? I'M SICK OF CLEANING!

Olive

Dear Olive,

I've added you and your baby to my prayer list. Just tell your mother-in-law that if it wasn't for those few crumbs on the floor every once in a while, the roaches and mice, which most likely have taken over the cupboards, closets, and any other dark area in your home, would most likely starve to death.

Love, Kisses, and Trailer Park Wishes,
Ruby Ann Boxcar

Siblings

Dear Ruby Ann Boxcar,

Let me start off by simply saying that I do not live in a mobile home, however I am a big fan of yours. With that said, here is my problem. My youngest brother seems to think that simply because I'm the oldest in the family, he can call me at all hours of the day when he finds himself in a jam, or a situation arises. He even has the nerve to call me late at night, needing my help, when my wife and I are sound asleep. Ms. Boxcar, I love my brother, and I will always be there for him, but most of the time, those after-midnight calls could easily wait until after the sun has risen. My wife and I are fighting because of his early A.M. calls, but I'm afraid that if I tell him to wait until the next day to pick up the phone or stop by, he will think that I don't want to be bothered by him. That couldn't be further from the truth. So what should I do?

Sleepy in Cincinnati

Dear Sleepy,

Lord, hon, don't I know the weight of your load that you've been forced to bear. Remember, I do have a sister. Mind you, she is a little older than me, but whenever she needs help, she's either slurrin' at me over the phone or poundin' on my trailer door. Why, just the other night this blood-curdlin' scream came from her trailer. Figurin' that once again one of her boyfriends for the night had somehow managed to sober up quick enough to turn on the bedroom light and see my sister clad in nothin' but a teddy, no one jumped up and threw their clothes on to run over and see if she needed help. After all, it was 4:00 o'clock in the mornin'. Well, soon after, my telephone started to ring off the wall. When I finally managed to reach over and answer it, I was greeted with yells of "Help me, sister, help me," on the other end. It was Donna Sue, all right, and she was horrified, panicked, and three sheets to the wind. After I managed to calm her down a bit, I asked her what the problem was. Well, she said that she'd just gotten home from a long night at work, and on her way in, she tripped over a kitchen chair and landed on the floor. She said she was hurt real bad, and that there was blood everywhere. And then she started yellin' for me to come quick, and to call an ambulance. Bein' the good carin' sister that I am, I woke up my husband and told him to go over and check on Donna Sue. Needless to say, at 4:00 A.M. his reply was less than Baptist, so I got out of bed, checked my makeup and hair, threw on a robe, and made my way through the cold blackness of the night to my sister's trailer. Since the ambulances don't run after midnight over by where we live on account of the hospital and emergency room closin' from 12:00 A.M. till 7:00 A.M. every night, I didn't try to call the ambulance. If it was bad, I'd just get my husband, Dew, to help me load her up in the back of the truck and take her over to the vet, who does take late-night emergency calls for an extra $5 on top of his normal $10 fee. Of course I'd throw her bedspread in the truck bed, 'cause the last thing I'd want to do is get bloodstains in my new truck. Well, long story short, after havin' several after-hours rounds with the other Blue Whale girls over to the Blue Whale Strip Club where she works, the old cow came back home, tripped, fell on the floor, and busted open a bottle of red wine she'd sneaked out from the bar at work. Her and her floor were covered with red wine, which she'd drunkenly mistaken for blood. In all actuality, the only things that had suffered serious damage were that wine bottle and the part of the dented-in kitchen floor where she'd landed. And of course she was fine. So I explained to her what had obviously happened, told her good night, and then headed back home. As I walked out her trailer door she thanked me for comin' over to check on her and then started suckin' up the kitchen floor with straw. So as you can see, in the words of my favorite president and a good old Arkansas boy, I can feel your pain.

My advice for you would be to do what I've done ever since that late-night red wine drama. Simply remove or shut off your bedroom phone, and regardless of how cold it might be outside, sleep with your head a little closer to the box fan at night. Sure, you might wake up a little clogged up or feelin' sneezy, but you'll be well rested regardless of what kind of tragedy might have fallen upon your loved ones in the middle of the night.

> Love, Kisses, and Trailer Park Wishes,
> Ruby Ann Boxcar

Dear Ruby Ann,

My sister is having a potluck bar-BEE-q party for her son's high school graduation. But anyone with half a brain knows that her son is at least two or three years away from graduating from anything. I know she's just having this party 'cause she wants to show off her new bar-BEE-q grill! And she's hoping for gifts (she told me)—cash to be precise—to pay for that new bar-BEE-q grill. I don't want to attend and support her bad behavior, but if I don't go I know that everyone in the park will think I'm just jealous of that new grill. Please give me some advice.

> Bertha Largechest

Dear Bertha,

Let me set you straight on the correct spellin' for both the grill your sister has as well as the kind of party that she plans on throwin'. It's a BBQ party and a BBQ grill, and I should know since I wrote a whole dang book on the topic. And the last thing I want is for someone to think that one of my fans is an idiot just 'cause they're spellin' ain't no good.

When it comes to your question about supportin' the BBQ that your sister is throwin' in order to raise money to pay off the new grill itself, let me give you a two-word answer. Shut up! It's that simple and complex. So what if she wants to charge people—after all, they are gettin' somethin' to eat as well as some time to socialize with their neighbors and friends. And who cares if her son is graduatin' or not?

I'm sure this whole event will give him the attention he is most likely cravin' especially when it comes from his very own family. So just shut up about the whole thing, let your sister, her son, and that new grill enjoy some of the spotlight for a little while, and arrive on time with a covered dish in your happy little hands. And if you still think you got to show your true feelin's for the whole event, just pretend later in the night that you've gotten food poisonin' from one of the items. After all, there ain't nothin' that will throw a wet blanket on a good-time eatin' party like the horrific cry of "food poison." So there, you got your bread and it was buttered on both sides for you.

> Love, Kisses, and Trailer Park Wishes,
> Ruby Ann Boxcar

Dear Ruby Ann,

Thank you for the chance to have you shed some light on a family problem. My brother is living with the Antichrist. Everyone in our family calls her the AC, including my eighty-year-old grandmother. She has an extremely foul mouth and has had protective services take away three of her four kids. This woman would rather sit in the car than come in the house to look you in the face. Do we have to continue to invite her to family events and Christian holidays? And if we do . . . what is a good gift for the Antichrist?

> Enthusiastically yours,
> Anonymous in Northern California

Dear Anonymous,

Just remember that regardless of where they might hang from the family tree, blood is always thicker than water, unless money or food are involved. Of course you got to invite her to your gatherin's. If she chooses to stay out in the car, then so be it. Leave her behind out there for hours if that's where she wants to stay durin' the gatherin'. Just don't ever give her the opportunity to be able to say to your brother, "See, I told you those people hated me and don't want me in their homes," 'cause if you do, then she'll have an excuse to pressure your brother into stayin' away from y'all. So make sure that she is always the first invited, regardless if she decides to come in or not.

When it comes to gift givin', I don't care who the person is, nothin' says, "Hey, you mean the world to me," like a Don Knotts movie. Personally I've found that nothin' will turn a frown upside down faster than my all-time favorite *The Ghost and Mister Chicken*. Not only will your gift bring hours of fun, but when that world-class thespian, Mr. Don Knotts, is involved, you know a good time will be had by all even if one of 'em happens to be the demon seed of Satan.

Love, Kisses, and Trailer Park Wishes,
Ruby Ann Boxcar

The Rest of the Clan

Dear Ruby Ann,

We've got thirty-three people in our clan and I buy Xmas gifts for everybody, beginning in June. Costs a bundle, including shipping, as everybody lives somewhere else. Last Xmas I hurt two grandkids' feelings (I bought a too juvenile book for one teen and a doll for a pre-teenybopper, and both cried). Should I quit buying gifts altogether? I'm fed up.

A Granny in Tears Too

Dear Granny in Tears Too,

I'm so sorry to hear how upset you are. You really shouldn't beat yourself to death on this, after all, mistakes happen, and isn't gift givin' all about the thought and not the gift? With that said, my dear, what kind of senile old woman are you that would buy a doll for a pre-teen? Good Lord, woman, don't you ever see these kids? Is the only time you hear from 'em is when you wait for them to sing your praises 'cause you were able to read the calendar and send 'em a Christmas card and gift? Like I said earlier, it's the thought that matters, and obviously you didn't put much thought into what you gave. If you start your Christmas shoppin' in June, then I'd think you'd be able to get at least some of the gifts right, but it sounds like you struck out twice in one swing. Maybe next year you should try and do what Santa Claus does, ask 'em what all they want, and then pick the cheapest gift. It may not be the best gift that they get, but at least it will be somethin' they want.

And speakin' of gifts, ten random items from one of them dollar stores don't make for one nice gift. If you want to give a nice gift, then do just that instead of givin' ten pieces of junk to a nice person. And if your grand babies want something from one of them Disney movies, then for goodness sakes, check the dang item for the word "Disney" printed somewhere on it. I don't care if it says "Little Mermaid," "Jungle Book," "Beauty and the Beast," or if it's shaped like a mouse. If it don't say "Disney" on it, then you might as well be given that kid a stick, 'cause they'll play with that knock-off item about as much as they would with the stick.

So, basically, remember one thing, if you're gonna take the time to give gifts, then for cryin' out loud, do it right or everybody that ends up with one of your lame presents is gonna hate you. I hope this helps you this year with your gift giving.

Love, Kisses, and Trailer Park Wishes,
Ruby Ann Boxcar

Dear Ruby Ann,

My cousin really needs a kidney but mine is already listed for sale on eBay. Which is really thicker . . . blood or money?

K Ray

Dear K Ray,

As I've stated before, blood is always thicker than water unless money or food are involved. With that said, it all turns around once the life of a family member is concerned. In that case, blood is thicker than money. So what I'd do if I was you, would be to go ahead and keep my kidney on eBay, put a cheap ad in your newspaper offerin' to pay a matchin' kidney donor an amount that is half of what you eventually get from your eBay sale. This way your cousin gets the donor's kidney, that donor gets enough money to buy groceries for his family, and you've still pulled in a profit from your own kidney. It's a win/win for everybody.

Love, Kisses, and Trailer Park Wishes,
Ruby Ann Boxcar

Family Gatherin's

Dear Ruby Ann,

I find my family's annual reunion quickly approaching, and as usual I am filled with anxiety. How many aunts will ask me, "When are you getting married?" How many cousins will inquire after any girlfriends I may have?

My questions are how is it appropriate to inform the relatives that I am gay? Is that a subject—like politics and religion—that I should not bring up at a huge family gathering? Also, I have an incredible new boyfriend who just takes my breath away. Is it fair to him and to the family to bring him along and spring him on them in such a manner? What's your take on the proper etiquette of such a thing?

Anxious,
MJ

Dear MJ,

Hon, I think you might just be readin' too much into this whole thing about how your family is gonna react. For example, my sister, Donna Sue, is happy and gay, and she ain't got no man in her life. Well, not one that wants to marry her right now. She finally set all us family members down and said, "Look, y'all, I am happy bein' single and ain't plannin' on gettin' married anytime soon, so please stop askin' me when I plan on gettin' hitched." Of course once her feelin's were known, we respected them. One of the reasons for this was that in our minds if she did find Mr. Right, most likely her children would turn out to be dysfunctional mutant freaks after all the booze she's drank for over the past forty years. I'm sure if you just tell your family the same thing, then you won't have no problems with 'em.

As far as your cousins askin' about your girlfriends, I don't see no problem with that at all, especially when you take into consideration the terrible datin' pool that's out there right now. I know that I got several girlfriends who I try to pawn off when I meet a nice man that I think would be perfect for them. All your cousins are doin' is tryin' to get you to set them up on a date with one of your gal pals. As long as they are single, I'm afraid that they are gonna always be askin' you that question. So get used to it, and try to help 'em out whenever possible.

When it comes to introducin' your boyfriend to the family, well, I think it's a mistake. After all, here you are on one hand sayin,' "Stop askin' me when I'm gettin' married," and then in the same breath you're sayin', "But I am seein' somebody who could turn out to be Mr. Right." I suggest that you talk to your family at the reunion first, and wait until a later date for them to meet your boyfriend. After all, if he starts feelin' the pressure from your family to ask you to marry him, he might just hightail it right out of your life. You sure don't want that now, do you?

By the way, does MJ stand for Mary Jane or Mary Joe? Just curious.

Love, Kisses, and Trailer Park Wishes,
Ruby Ann Boxcar

Dear Ruby Ann,

I have a question. I have a second cousin, who isn't very attractive and lives in small-town western Oklahoma. She invites us to a family reunion yearly at the school cafeteria there, and tells us it's an all-you-can-eat buffet, then proceeds to tell us to bring our own meat, vegetables, breads, and desserts. She supplies coffee and water, but absolutely no pop. She tells us repeatedly that there will be absolutely no pop provided, so if one must indulge in such things, they'll have to bring their own. Ruby, all-knowing goddess of all things, Is their some religious, moral, or ethical thing about soft drinks that I am not aware of?

Signed,
Hankering for a Dr Pepper in Oklahoma

Dear Hankerin',

Let me start off by answerin' your question about the soda pop first. Yes, there are some faiths that don't allow soda or at least not the ones with caffeine in 'em, to be consumed by the faithful. Can you imagine goin' to your deathbed without ever havin' the joys that come from a sip of RC Cola or Dr Pepper? Of course with the caffeine-free Dr Pepper and RC Cola they got out now, everybody can enjoy a cold one. Well, almost everybody. With that said, there are still some folks who think that the carbonation is bad for you. Those are the same people that believe you can get cancer from cookin' food in a microwave oven. Mind you, these folks say it's OK to just reheat your food in a microwave, 'cause you only get cancer from it if you are actually cookin' the food in it and not just warmin' it up. Then you got those folks who will tell you just before they take a drink from their great big glass of sweet tea that "soda pop will rot your teeth out." Some people are just bizarre and there ain't nothin' you can do about it. Personally, if I was you, I'd lay down a big plastic tarp in my trunk and fill it with ice and soda pop. I'd then drive it up to the back door of the school cafeteria and pop the trunk for all to enjoy. Let that crazy cousin and her kids be the only ones not enjoyin' a soda. That'll teach her Dr Pepper–hatin' behind a lesson. And while you're at it, why not whip up the Dr Pepper Salad recipe from my first book, *Ruby Ann's Down Home Trailer Park Cookbook,* and rename it somethin' like Simply Surprise Salad. Wait till she fills her face with a big helpin' and then asks you for the recipe before revealin' that the secret ingredient is two cans of Dr Pepper.

Speakin' of your cousin, I couldn't help but notice that you don't think highly of her at all. You mention how she is unattractive, which ain't got nothin' to do with the rest of your letter. I can't help but wonder if there ain't more to this relationship that y'all have. Maybe you're jealous of her 'cause she's able to gain access to a school cafeteria once a year? Or perhaps it's the fact that she's actually able to get the family to get together? If y'all wasn't cousins, I'd say the tension y'all seem to have was sexual. Of course you did say you live in Oklahoma, so maybe it is. Regardless, it's time y'all just let it go and free yourself from all the hate or whatever it is that fills both your bein's. Just blow it out! Get rid of it! Begone, mean spirits! Just repeat over and over, "I love my cousin." Let it go! Release it! Push those mean thoughts right out of your body, and then get in your car, go to the event, and secretly add some white vinegar or pickle juice to the tea and water containers.

> Love, Kisses, and Trailer Park Wishes,
> Ruby Ann Boxcar

Dear Ruby Ann,

I have a big problem. My grandparents seem to think we need to get the whole family together four or five times a year. This would not be so bad except that my grammy likes to drink, and when she ties one on (which is every time the family gets together) she likes to do a little bit of a striptease. It all started a few years back when, at a family reunion, we all went out to a beautiful lake for boating, barbecuing, and bonding . . . and Grammy started dipping into the watermelon schnapps and went on a mission. She ended up getting everyone within three camping lots from us to all go skinny-dipping in the lake with her. Needless to say, park rangers came and took Grammy away, and we had to leave the reunion early to go bail her out of jail for indecent (and I might add wrinkled) exposure. Love her to death, but it's starting to get a little embarrassing, and we're going broke for all the bail we have to raise. Any advice you could offer would really save my family any more public humiliation.

Respectfully,
Grammy Complex

Dear Grammy Complex,

It seems to me that you got two choices in the matter. You can either put her down, which I don't advise, or stop bailin' her out. I'd say just stop comin' to the reunion, but all that is gonna do is hurt her feelin's, and since she gets others involved already, she'll just continue with or without y'all. So I say leave her in jail for a while. Simply tell her that nobody can come up with the bail money immediately, but y'all are workin' on it. I got a feelin' that after a week or so of sharin' a cell with a hardened criminal, your granny is gonna come out a changed woman. Of course, part of that change could be that she begins cuttin' her hair short and starts rollin' her own cigarettes, but who cares, just as long as she keeps her clothes on.

Love, Kisses, and Trailer Park Wishes,
Ruby Ann Boxcar

Chapter 2

Children

Them punks don't even think about my yard anymore when they're out lookin' for trouble and things to steal. If it's done right, you can easily hook up fifteen or twenty assorted lawn statues to just one well-hid semitruck battery.

Y'all know that show called *Kids Say the Darndest Things* with Art Linkletter and then later on with Bill Cosby? You know, the one where the darlin' little children would be asked questions and they'd come up with the funniest little answers? Well, from the letters I get from y'all, the movie *The Omen* is much more closer to reality than that TV show. I'm tellin' you, some of y'all got kids that would make that pea-spittin', head-twirlin', sailor-talkin' gal from *The Exorcist* look like Shirley Temple in *Heidi*. There are times when I read your questions that I can't help but thank the good Lord that I had the sense to get my tubes tied when I did, and devote my attentions and affections to my dogs. And the funny part about the whole thing is that none of y'all think your kids are the mean ones. In your eyes your babies are nothin' more than little angels. Well, let me set y'all straight right here and now: When a bell rings, most of y'all's babies ain't gonna get their wings. Horns, maybe, but definitely no wings. If y'all don't heed my warnin's and strict advice, y'all are gonna be spendin' a lot of time on visitor's day down at your local corrections facility—if you catch my drift.

Of course there are some exceptions out there, folks who have good kids that tend to experience little problems from time to time. And that's just fine and natural. After all, there were only two perfect children in this world and they were Jesus and Sister Bertha from Lot #12 (she's just taken over as head of the book-burnin' committee, so please bear with me).

The important thing to remember for all you parents out there is this, children can be best raised if you treat 'em just like dogs. Make sure that you spend time with them, play games with 'em, bathe 'em and cut their hair, take 'em in to get their shots, feed 'em and make sure they got clean water, reward 'em with praise, and when they pee on the carpet, rub their noses in it. Too many of y'all just let your kids do somethin' bad and you don't rub their noses in it. You don't discipline with an iron hand, and I ain't talkin' about spankin', but simply correctin' 'em. Dogs will run right out in the street if you don't keep 'em on a line, and your children will do the same, run out into that street of life and get hit by a 1967 car of evil ways. Y'all have got to give your kids some kind of direction, just like you would if you was walkin' a dog on a leash. 'Cause folks, if you don't take care of 'em now, they're gonna turn on you and go for the jugular.

So as you read the letters that I've included in this chapter, think of your own babies. Ask yourself questions. Could these kids be mine? Are there things I need to discuss with my children? Should I be a little stricter? Is it too late to turn them over for adoption?

And now, on to your letters.

Your Little Angels

Dear Ruby Ann,

My son is fourteen years old and I think he is going through puberty because he is always looking at his female cousins in a strange way. I am very concerned that if I do something wrong he may turn into a serial killer or something. Is there anything I can do to assist him through his growth period without scarring him for life?

Signed,
Mrs. Grace

Dear Mrs. Grace,

I don't know if y'all's cousins are anything like mine, but if they are, I'd suggest you start off by gettin' that boy of yours some much-needed eyeglasses. You know, what this boy is feelin' is as natural as, oh, say, processed cheese. Stoppin' his need to look would be like stoppin' his need to drink water. And even though the last thing he would want is for you to be tellin' him who he can and can't look at, you still need to help guide him in his viewin' directions. In other words, take him some place where he can look at females that he ain't related to. I'd suggest that you enroll him in a sewin' class or even encourage him to take home economics at his local school. I know that the drama clubs in most schools are also a great place to go if you want to be around women. And fashion classes at Vo Tech are almost always filled with attractive girls that he can get to know and ogle. Best of luck, and please keep me posted on how your boy's journey into manhood advances.

Love, Kisses, and Trailer Park Wishes,
Ruby Ann Boxcar

Dear Ruby Ann,

I have three-year-old, five-year-old, and six-year-old daughters. And they all take a bath together. Every time I put them in the bath the youngest one poops in the tub. Can you please give me advice on how to break her of this habit.

Helpless

Dear Helpless,

This one is pretty easy. Just feed the youngest one about a half a pound of Velveeta cheese two hours before bathtime. Problem solved.

Love, Kisses, and Trailer Park Wishes,
Ruby Ann Boxcar

Dear Ruby Ann,

I've had three husbands, six sons, and now seven grandchildren. My grandchildren want to know how come they have three grandpas with me and only one with their other grandma. How should I answer them?

JN

Dear JN,

Just tell 'em the reason that they got three grandpas with you and only one with the other grandma is 'cause you got taste.

Love, Kisses, and Trailer Park Wishes,
Ruby Ann Boxcar

Dear Ruby Ann,

My child was sent home from school with head lice. Do you recommend using Hartz flea and tick dip, or will a onetime application of Frontline work just as well?

Eddie

Dear Eddie,

Listen, hon, don't take them head lice lightly. Go seek professional help as quick as you can. Trust me on this one. My niece, Lulu Bell, of Lot #8 still has the scars from her first couple of cases of head lice. And now that her hair is startin' to thin out so she looks somethin' like a bad imported baby doll, you can see the marks where them little critters ate her head up like it was a melon ball. Of course with her recorded IQ, I guess technically it is.

Love, Kisses, and Trailer Park Wishes,
Ruby Ann Boxcar

Dear Ruby Ann.

My daughter developed an allergy to our cats. The doctor said to get rid of the cats. My sons want to keep the cats and get rid of their sister. What should I do?

Thank you,
Carol Kluz

Dear Carol,

This one is simple. Get a dog! You sons will fall in love real fast with the dog, and they'll forget about those cats, wherever they might be. If your daughter turns out to be allergic to the dog, then I'd suggest boardin' school. That or send her off to live with a relative.

Love, Kisses, and Trailer Park Wishes,
Ruby Ann Boxcar

Dear Ruby Ann,

I have been a single parent of six ever since my beloved husband passed on to glory several years ago. All of the children are grown now, and some even have darling children of their own. My problem is, I can't get several of them to leave the nest. I thought about marrying a big hairy biker-type man to run them off, but I would like to have some kind of a relationship with them in my old age and am not sure that I would want a relationship with him in my old age! What can I do?

Signed me,
Mama Stahlman

Dear Mama Stahlman,

Thank you for trustin' me with your situation. I got to warn you that this is gonna be a long one, so brace yourself. Now, let me tell you that it's time, sweet thing, that you either do your business or get out of the bathroom so somebody else can. You've brought this wretched problem on yourself by lettin' them kids run wild and do whatever they wanted to all in the name of good motherin'. Well, the inmates have taken over the asylum, as they say, and the only way you're gonna retake the facility is to fill up the place with smoke. Mind you, you don't want to burn it down, but rather simply make 'em think it's on fire. You do this by gatherin' up all your babies, includin' any of 'em that don't live with you, and you ask them that have a job the followin' question: "Do y'all hope to spend the rest of your life workin' the same job you're workin' right now for the same amount of pay?" Most of 'em are gonna say no. The next question goes to those kids of yours who ain't workin', and it is: "Do y'all hope to spend the rest of your life livin' on the same amount of money that you live off of now?" They'll most likely say no as well. Then ask all of 'em if they would like to do somethin' more with their lives, live out the dreams that they dare to dream." When they say yes to that, come back with, "Good, 'cause so does your momma, which means that things are gonna have to change. You see, your momma is tired of making the same money that she makes and would love to fulfill that dream that she has always dreamt. In other words, your momma has decided to take some correspondence courses. Yes, in just a few short years I'll have my degree in fashion merchandizing and computer repair." Now this is the point where your kids will find their jaws startin' to drop. Some of you might even find the little ones statin' a fact.

"But, Momma, you ain't got no computer."

"That's right, which means I'm gonna have to eventually buy one," you reply. "And since I'm gonna need a computer as well as money to pay for my courses, I'm gonna have to start charging all of you that live here rent."

"But, Momma . . ."

"But nothin'. I birthed all you kids and raised you to be what you are today. I gave up on most of my dreams so y'all could follow yours, and even threw away any chance at bein' a runway model just so you kids would have a mother here waiting for you when you came home from school. And now that all of you are old enough to hold down a job, it's my turn to live, which means I will be collecting $275 on the first of every month for rent and an additional $50 a week for food. My classes are gonna cost me a lot of money, and I got to get that computer as well."

"But I don't have a job," one of 'em argues.

"Then I suggest you get one, 'cause I can't afford to support you anymore. Plus, you see, I had a dream last night where Ms. Sally Struthers was up on a stage and she called my name. As I approached that outstanding actress and all-around female role model, she pulled out a pen and signed two diplomas. She then handed 'em to me along with a screwdriver and ring of fabric color swatches and wished me the best of luck. That was when I woke up and realized that the day had come for me to finally live out my dream. So those of you who are living under my roof will either move out, which I understand, or come up with $475 a month for rent and food. I love all of you, but it's Momma's turn to live."

Now that should do it. Just make sure you force all of 'em to follow those rules. No one, but no one gets to break them there rules that you just set down. Of course you ain't got to go to no correspondence school. If anyone asks you about it, just tell 'em for the first couple of months that you are waiting for the packet to arrive in the mail. Then durin' the next couple of months, buy a new fashion magazine and put it on your coffee table. When the kids visit and ask how the classes are goin', just point to the cover and say, "I suggested the earrings." Later on, go to the thrift store and buy the cheapest, oldest-lookin' computer that you can get. See if they got one that don't even work that is already in pieces and see if they'll take $10 for it. Put that in one of the spare bedrooms, and claim you've been workin' on it for the past three months. Of course, if anybody comes to you with questions about their computer, tell 'em that it would be unethical for you to give them any advice until you got your frameable signed diploma. Within a few months your kids will be out of your hair, and your relationship with them will blossom shortly. They will eventually forget about the classes since they now have their own lives to live, but if the subject does come back up, simply say that you've decided to take a semester off or are thinkin' about switchin' your degree. That should do it for you. Good luck.

Love, Kisses, and Trailer Park Wishes,
Ruby Ann Boxcar

Them Other Brats

Dear Ruby Ann,

If your dog bites a neighbor's rotten kid, is it the dog's fault for doing what any sensible creature would do—biting a kid who richly deserves it, and how do you prove it in court?

P.H.

Dear P.H.,

I don't let kids around my three little girls simply 'cause children can upset dogs so easily by pullin' on their ears or messin' with their tails or messin' up their boufonts. But to be honest with you, I'm all for the dog, and if you got to go to court over such a case, I suggest you get a sedative from your vet for your dog. This way when you take your little one into the courtroom, he or she will be laid back, relaxed, and look extremely passive. Tell the judge that your dog is always this way, which is why you were surprised that he bit the child. Obviously, as the court can see, that kid must have done something mean and vicious to your poor Lassie. Now this will only work a few times. After that, you might want to think about movin' to the country with dear doggie.

> Love, Kisses, and Trailer Park Wishes,
> Ruby Ann Boxcar

Dear Ruby Ann,

My Latrel, whom I call "Momma's little precious" has been getting teased by other fourth-grade students because he carries a briefcase to school. Now, I spent years teaching Momma's little precious to be organized, efficient, and professional. (I want him good and trained so he can get one of them solid government jobs, like a mailman or something, when he's all grown. They have the best benefits; I'm always telling him to look into the benefits when applying for a job. Plus, he'll be able to take care of me in my old age with a good job.)

Well, now, he wants to use a cruddy old backpack, just like the other kids. It'll be the ruin of him, I just know it. There goes the benefits package, my comfort in my old age—I can just see disaster riding down the train track of life. What can I do to stop him from listening to those darn kids?

> Signed,
> Momma's Little Precious Washed Up at Ten Years Old

Dear Washed Up Momma,

Hon, don't you worry about your son. You can turn this setback into a step forward. Just ask him if he enjoys carryin' the new bag, and then ask him if he would like to carry that new bag around every day. More than likely he will say yes, and if he does, then tell him that postmen get to carry a big bag around all day long too. As a matter of fact, they even get to play with doggies from time to time while they work. Wouldn't he like a job where he can carry around a bag and play with doggies too? That should get your young one back on track. If that don't do it, then just dress him all in pink one time and send him off to school. Trust me, he won't never listen to what those darn kids at school say ever again after that.

> Love, Kisses, and Trailer Park Wishes,
> Ruby Ann Boxcar

Dear Ruby Ann,

My neighbor's son, Randy, has decided he's too busy while playing to stop and use the facilities. He keeps relieving himself under my magnolia bush! Whenever I go to that side of my trailer, or take a walk around to see my magnolia, I can always tell if Randy has been there. One time, I even caught him under the bush with his pants down around his ankles. I tried talking to my neighbor about it, but she just shakes her head and says, "Boys will be boys." What am I to do?

> Signed,
> My Neighbor Stinks and Her Kid Stinks Worse

Dear Stinks Worse,

Well, it seems to me that you got four choices, all of which will eventually work to solve your problem.

1. Call the police and have them cite your neighbor for not keepin' her animal on a leash, which is what he is if he is using the yard as a bathroom.

2. When you find that your neighbor's kid has left you a present under your magnolia, get a shovel and sling the gift back into his yard.

3. Hook up an electric fence wire around the magnolia and wait for the screams.

4. Just go pee on your neighbor's begonias.

> Love, Kisses, and Trailer Park Wishes,
> Ruby Ann Boxcar

Dear Ruby Ann,

My neighbor has been a dear friend of mine ever since I plopped my trailer down on blocks next door. She even let me tie into her septic tank for nearly six months till I could afford to dig my own with my late husband's insurance money. The problem is her six kids are drivin' me crazy and she won't do a thing to make 'em mind. They are always shootin' at somethin' or blowin' somethin' up. They've blown up four of my mailboxes with firecrackers or shotguns. My nerves are on edge from the gunshots and explosions. She won't make them go to school or bathe or anything.

I think that whole family is mental and I can't take any more. Ruby

Ann, what should I do? I can't afford to move and I'm afraid those dang kids are gonna kill us all. If I call the police on 'em there's no tellin' what those kids will do to me or my trailer.

Please help!

Afraid to Sleep in Seattle

Dear Afraid,

My goodness, hon, you do have a terrible problem, but not to worry, 'cause I got a few suggestions for you. First off, I would go to church and pray for help from God. Ask him for a twister, a lightnin' strike, or some other act that wouldn't be covered by their insurance, in order to get them out of your trailer park. If he don't answer your prayer within a week, then it simply means that he has decided to "help those who help themselves" in this situation.

So you have to take care of this situation yourself. I'd suggest that you find the nearest biker bar and see if anyone needs a little extra cash. Mind you, don't pay a lot 'cause these fellas would most likely do it for free, but $20 or $30 would be about right accordin' to my neighbor Little Linda, who's dated some of these men before. Anyways, either have 'em tip your neighbors trailer over once a week until they move, or ask 'em to show up late at night with a truck and haul that whole dang thing out of there and drive it to the next county.

Regardless of which option you choose, I'm sure that once you follow my advice, your problems should be solved in no time at all, and you can go back to livin' that widow woman life that you've so longed to enjoy.

Love, Kisses, and Trailer Park Wishes,
Ruby Ann Boxcar

Dear Ruby Ann,

I have a problem and I just don't know what to do about it. I've become a free spirit around the trailer since my ninth husband and I went our separate ways a few years back. I don't know why, but I've found that I get a better night's sleep in the "natural." Well, you see, the other night I thought I heard some noises outside along the back of my trailer home, so I jumped up, grabbed a flashlight, and made my way to my back door without turning on a light. Without thinking of my own safety, I opened that back door as hard as I could, knocking these three small boys, about eight or nine years old, down the back steps and onto each other. I shined my flashlight on their faces, but they were so distorted with what had to be fear that I couldn't make a one of them out. Well, they took off running like frightened rabbits. That was when I realized I was standing there in the open doorway buck naked. Mind you, none of my neighbors were up or at least none of them were outside. So I quickly closed my back door and locked it. I wanted to call the police since those kids were obviously trying to break into my trailer, but at the same time I was afraid that they might end up arresting me for indecent exposure. I'm sixty-seven years old and the last thing I need is to go to jail. But I don't want those kids to lead a life of crime when they grow up just because I didn't call the police when they were young. Ruby Ann, do you think I did the right thing?

Signed,
Concerned About the Kids

Dear Concerned,

Hon, I got a feelin' that them little boys have most likely been punished enough and will grow up with those scars and nightmares for the rest of their unnatural lives. By the way, that look that you called fear was most likely more along the lines of horror and disgust, but don't quote me on that.

Love, Kisses, and Trailer Park Wishes,
Ruby Ann Boxcar

Chapter 3

Neighbors

Not only have I got dents in my trailer skirtin', but almost all my pink flamingos are discolored and rusted.

You know, I've had pretty good luck over the years when it comes to neighbors at the High Chaparral Trailer Park. Sure some of 'em are crazier than loons, but they're all good people who wouldn't cause no harm to you, and would rather eat snakes than do you wrong, unless of course you do 'em wrong first. But I didn't realize how good these folks were until me and my husband, Dew, got our holiday trailer in the elite part of Commerce City, Colorado.

Now let me just say that I can't go into no kind of details about location or neighbors names or nothin' like that when it comes to my Commerce City trailer, on account of the fact that I had to sign an agreement when me and my husband, Dew, moved in that promises I'll keep my mouth shut. I guess they've had other celebrities move in the trailer park in the past and they don't want folks drivin' around the park at all hours of the night tryin' to spot my home. And you really can't blame 'em. After all, the last thing I'd want to do if I was them is to have to throw somethin' on just so I can answer the door, only to find out that it's some tourist lookin' for where "Ruby Ann lives." So I'm fine with that. What I ain't fine with is the way some of my neighbors *are,* or should I say *have been.* You see, we got our quad-wide trailer home—they wouldn't let us build up so we built out—settin' right on the inside corner of the park, so there's only one lot next to us. On the other side is the swimmin' pool, which, by the way, if you ever want to bring a loud nightly skinny-dippin' pool party to an end, dumpin' a big old bucket of leeches in the water before the festivities begin is sure to do the trick. You should have heard the screams! Anyways, back to what I was sayin'

81

about the lot next to me. When we moved in, there was no neighbor there at all, as a matter of fact, there wasn't even a lot. But as Denver and Commerce City kept growin', the people who own the park decided to turn that area into an additional space for a trailer. As you can guess, me and my husband, Dew, weren't at all thrilled with that idea, but we understood.

Well, within days of the first neighbor movin' in, our understandin' turned to frustration. They had kids, and they was the devil's seeds. I mean these kids were just unruly and didn't listen to nothin'. One day I caught the little tykes playin' around my propane tank, and when I told 'em not to touch it, they cursed at me. Now, I ain't talkin' teenagers. These kids were four or five years old at tops, and already talkin' like that. Why, you'd have thought you was watchin' an episode of *The Osbornes* with the way them little ones swore at me. Well, I marched their little behinds over to their trailer and told their parents what they'd said. Needless to say, the parents weren't much better, and they told me to mind my own business. Mind my business, all right. The next day I watered my yard down until it was mud, went over and told the parents how sorry I was for my behavior the day before, and asked if their kids could come over and play in my yard. They were happy to get their demonic offspring out of their house. As you can guess, the little ones couldn't resist playin' in my yard with all the mud, and after they was covered from head to toe in muck, I told 'em to go and hide under their trailer, and I'd be right there with some cookies. Well, I brought 'em cookies all right, along with an empty box of Fruit Loops, two spoons, a half-used roll of toilet paper, and I threw it all under their trailer, along with the toys them kids kept leavin' in my yard. Then I ran off and called the police. I anonymously reported that I suspected my neighbors had been makin' their kids live under the trailer. Well, long story short, the police showed up, they hauled their butts off, and the lot was vacant two days later. The last thing you want to do is tell me to mind my own business. Needless to say, we've had more neighbors move in to that lot since, but for some odd reason, none of 'em have stayed very long.

And now, on to your letters.

The Good

Dear Ruby Ann,

I think I live next door to heaven because my neighbors are angels. They are both retired and just as kind as can be. When my husband and I moved in, they brought us a big basket of homemade muffins over as a welcome gift. During the summer the wife always comes knocking with a baked pie at least once a week, and hot chocolate and fresh cookies during the winter months. When her husband mows the yard, he always heads over to our place and mows ours as well. And you wouldn't believe how many snowy mornings I've awoken to see that our sidewalk has been shoveled. They are just too kind, which is probably why I feel so bad about my question. Both my husband and I work from home, which is wonderful; however, we tend to be frisky people. Basically, it seems lately that regardless of what time of day we decide to be an active married couple, so to speak, one of our angels always rings the doorbell right in the middle of the activity. At first we just jumped up and answered the door, but then we both decided that we would just pretend we didn't hear it. Our little angels just continued to ring the doorbell or knock on the door until we answered it. So last week my husband decided to simply park our cars down the street so that they couldn't see we were at home. Sure enough they came by. They continued to ring and ring the doorbell for almost ten minutes. Now, normally in our case, ten minutes is more than enough time for us to finish what we are doing, but with that ding-dong ringing through the halls, it wasn't long enough. Finally they stopped and went away. Well, you could only imagine our horror when just three or four minutes later the fire and police department came crashing through our front door to find us in the game room without a pool stick or a billiard ball nearby. It seemed our neighbors had spotted our cars down the street, so when we didn't answer they assumed there might be foul play involved and they called the police and fire department. And as you can guess, we haven't seen the dear souls in almost a week. Ruby Ann, what should we do?

Signed,
So Embarrassed

Dear Embarrassed,

First off, you might want to have somebody professional come out and rebalance that pool table of yours.

Second, I'd suggest y'all might want to make up a gift basket with things that they might like. Put in some gift certificates for the movies and a restaurant along with some fruit and maybe even a cheesecake. Add a bottle of champagne as well. Take it over to them and tell them how important they are in your lives, and then thank them from the bottom of your hearts for everythin' they've done in the past. As you leave, make sure to hand them a piece of paper that says somethin' like "Please stop by any time. Our phone number is . . ." and leave it at that. They'll get the hint and you'll start gettin' the cookies and pies once again.

> Love, Kisses, and Trailer Park Wishes,
> Ruby Ann Boxcar

The Bad

Dear Ruby Ann,

While drivin' through my trailer park, I was busy puttin' on my lipstick and done run over one of the neighbor's dogs. Do I offer these folks a casserole, a sympathy card, or just pretend that dent has always been in my Chevy bumper and deny everything? Mind you, the dog seems to be just fine except for the fact that he has to lean on a trailer to pee.

> K.R.

Dear K.R.,

This is why I tell all you ladies to put the cosmetics on before you leave your trailer. The only woman that needs to apply lipstick outside of the comfort of her own home or a bathroom is one whose profession calls for her to spend a lot of time outside of the house at night.

Personally, if nobody has said nothin' about your horrific incident, I'd learn my lesson, give the poor people a friendly casserole or pie so that you feel better, sneak that dog away to the vet so he can secretly be examined, pay all costs that ensue, and keep your doggone eye on the road from now on. Oh, and dependin' on how big that dog is, you might want to make sure that all your trailer skirtin' is well attached.

Love, Kisses, and Trailer Park Wishes,
Ruby Ann Boxcar

Dear Ruby Ann,

Every time a tornado hits our trailer park, it seems like it always blows away the home of a neighbor whom I have lent some Tupperware to recently. How long after the tornado is it appropriate to wait to ask about my Tupperware (assuming of course they didn't get blown away with it). I mean, is it rude to come up to them while they are being interviewed for the news and ask about it?
Please tell me the proper interval.

Signed,
I Am Getting Poorer While My Tupperware Lady Is Getting Richer

Dear Getting Poorer,

Trust me when I say, I feel your plastic-ware pain. I can't tell you how many times I've had to replace the empty Cool Whip, Parkay margarine drums, or other "trailer plastic ware" containers that I've loaned out to Sister Bertha. Luckily, as I've reported in my other books, when a twister hits the High Chaparral Trailer Park, for some reason it usually takes only her trailer, sparin' me and my neighbors' homes. Anyways, I now simply write my name, address, and phone number on the outside bottoms of the containers in hopes that if I do loan them out to Sister Bertha, and a twister does hit, then maybe some kind soul will find them and return them. In the meantime, I ask for a cash deposit, which is what I'd suggest you do, for no more than the amount that it cost you to replace what you lend. Of course it would be un-Christian to charge any more than that unless, of course, they happen to be repeat offenders. In that case, you set your own price on that one. Good luck!

Love, Kisses, and Trailer Park Wishes,
Ruby Ann Boxcar

Dear Ruby Ann,

My family is having a reunion. My brothers insist that a keg of Old Milwaukee beer is plenty, but I think we should add some tasty boxed white zinfandel for the party. We always have Old Mil. Anyway, they're telling me I'm getting all snobby and whatnot cuz I want to offer some wine. I can't get them to shut up, and now the whole town is talkin' about me being uppity. What should I do?

Ardy Schwoop

Dear Ardy,

Not bein' a beer or wine drinker myself, I asked my dear older sister, Donna Sue, author of *Donna Sue's Down Home Trailer Park Bartending Guide,* to help out with this one. Accordin' to her, and she should know, you most likely are gonna need more than one keg. The way to figure this out is real simple. Donna Sue says to take the number of people you expect to have, we'll say forty, divide this by two since that's about how many people each keg will serve, and then have that many kegs on hand, which in our case would be twenty.

When it comes to the question about servin' wine, if I was you, I'd bring a box along with you for your own personal use. More than likely, people at the reunion will want to sample a little, so fill 'em up a clear plastic glass so everybody can see that you were right about other folks wantin' somethin' other than beer. And if it should happen that nobody asks you for a glass, simply ask one of your relatives to hold your glass for you so you can use both your hands to take a photo of 'em. Even if nobody else took even the smallest sip from your box, the photos will tell a different story. Make photocopies and pass 'em all over town. That should stop the uppity comments.

Love, Kisses, and Trailer Park Wishes,
Ruby Ann Boxcar

The Ugly

Dear Ruby Ann,

You've got to help me. My next-door neighbors in the duplex smell. I don't mean as in when I see them outside that they smell, but that there is a horrific odor that comes from their part of the duplex into our part of the duplex. It is the worst smell I have ever encountered in my life. I can't even describe it. But when my husband and I have guests over, they all find reasons to leave after the first five minutes. I don't want to start any trouble, and I hate confrontation. We told our landlord, but he says he can't smell anything when he comes over. What can I do?

Nauseated in Newark

Dear Nauseated,

As I see it, you only got three choices;

- Move.
- Check and make sure that in fact it is the neighbors that you are smellin'.
- Call the police and anonymously report that there's a dead body in your neighbor's house.

If none of these three appeal, maybe the followin' will help. There are many wonderfully scented potpourri recipes, and makin' potpourri can be both fun and entertainin'. It don't take much money to put together a nice fragrance that will not only mask the smell you're experiencin' but also brighten up your day. So regardless if you heat it up in a Crock-Pot or just leave it out in a bowl, be sure to enjoy the beauty of potpourri. Of course, personally, well, unless it's that Christmas stuff, I can't stand it. I'd rather have a nice fragrance candle, but I ain't the one with the odor problem in my house.

When you're makin' any of these potpourris, with the one exception bein' Donna Sue's simmerin' pot recipe, just put it in an empty jar, shake it up real good, and leave it alone. Turn it every four days, and then just leave it alone. Your homemade potpourri should be ready for use in about a month.

Donny's Lover Come Back to Me Potpourri

When it comes to stuff like this, Donny reminds me a lot of that real rugged fella with the beard that's got his own show on the Discovery Channel. His name slips me, but I sure like what he does.

7 cups red rosebuds and petals
2 cups purple globe amaranth
2 cups mauve wild orchids
2 cups pink rosebuds—boutons
2 cups uva ursi leaves
2 cups Burgundy Windmill pods
2 cups white statice flowers
2 cups chamomile
1 cup cinnamon chips, cut large
1 cup lemongrass
1 cup allspice
1 cup oak moss
½ cup rosemary
Freesia Essence oil, just a drop or two

For instructions, see the introduction to this section.

—DONNY OWENS, LOT #15

Lulu Bell's Dry Pie in the Sky Potpourri

This one just makes me hungry!

6 cups favorite dried flowers, mixed
2 tablespoons cinnamon
2 tablespoons noniodized picklin' salt
Apple Essence oil, as much as you personally like

For instructions, see the introduction to this section.

—LULU BELL BOXCAR, LOT #8

Donna Sue's Just Like David Simmerin' Pot Potpourri

Donna Sue named this after a fella she met durin' one of our New York City trips. He stole her heart, and she stole his innocence, along with cab fare to get back to her hotel.

6 tablespoons peppermint essence oil
1 tablespoon spearmint essence oil
1 tablespoon rosemary
1 tablespoon dried lemon peel
1 tablespoon dried lime peel
¼ stick licorice, diced into very small pieces

For instructions, see the introduction to this section.

—DONNA SUE BOXCAR, LOT #6

Ode to Me-Ma

God bless her, after only two weeks, the smell is a dead-on ringer for the old gal.

1 slice of baloney
1 Twinkie
½ banana
2 cups dried roses
½ cup apple vinegar
3 tablespoons grape jelly
2 tablespoons vanilla extract
1 tablespoon ointment, any kind
2 teaspoons ammonia

For instructions, see the introduction to this section. I don't really recommend that you try makin' this one though. Hardly anybody actually likes it—and it's a lot of work to make it and then just go an' have to throw it out.

—ME-MA, FORMERLY OF LOT #16

I do hope these help.

> Love, Kisses, and Trailer Park Wishes,
> Ruby Ann Boxcar

Dear Ruby Ann,

At what age does nudism cease to be an option? Please tell me so I can call the police on my neighbor.

> Signed,
> Almost Blind

Dear Almost Blind,

Nudism is somethin' that is part of life. It is natural, and even Christian, since our bodies come from the good Lord above, just as long as it's kept inside the trailer. So I would have to say that there is no age limit to runnin' around your trailer naked. With that said, let me tell you that I do believe that once people hit thirty-five they should hang up thicker curtains and make sure that they are pulled completely down from 6:00 P.M. to 10:00 A.M. durin' the week, and all day and night durin' the weekend.

> Love, Kisses, and Trailer Park Wishes,
> Ruby Ann Boxcar

And Worst Yet, the Political

Dear Ms. Boxcar,

I just found out my neighbor, who is a really nice woman, is a Republican, and I'm a Democrat. Every day she goes on about how wonderful the Republican Party is. What should I do?

> Queen of the Donkeys

Dear Queenie,

There are only two things that you can do. Pray for her, and if you have a Tupperware party, invite her over. With the kind of money she and them Republicans most likely got, your hostess gift could be real good, if you know what I mean, hon.

Love, Kisses, and Trailer Park Wishes,
Ruby Ann Boxcar

Chapter 4

Friends

"Momma, it looks like we're gonna need to put more duct tape on our trailer luggage."

you know, I'm the kind of person who will stand with a friend through thick and thin without waverin' in any direction, unless of course the media's involved, and then you're on your own. But to me a friendship is somethin' that you hold on to and cherish each and every day regardless of how much of a pain in the bottom that friend can be from time to time.

Why, I remember this one gal that I went to school with up at the Pangburn Academy of Beauty and Horse Shoeing way back when I was fresh out of high school and just livin' on my own. Her name was Whitney Lee, and she was so beautiful. Well, as you can guess, the two of us, bein' as attractive as we were, hit it off right from the start. We became best buddies. Of course she was much older than me, around twenty-three, and had recently moved to Searcy. She came down to the academy on account of gettin' a grant or somethin'. Well, we would set next to each other in class, and when it came time to pick partners for projects we selected each other, and even used to go out to eat every day durin' lunch break. We were near and dear friends. Then one night I had her over to my trailer to watch some TV. We had popcorn and RC Colas and just talked away like schoolgirls. And after an evenin' of good close friendship, she went on home and I hit the bed. It wasn't until the next mornin' that I notice one of my falls was missin'. You see, back in the sixties, I used to stack two falls on my head and then spray 'em down and tease 'em out till they wouldn't tease no more. Why, I had to avoid ceilin' fans like the plague. Anyways, I went to school that next Monday, and sure enough Whitney's hair had grown another foot. But bein' the good trailer park Baptist girl that I was, I didn't say a thing. Not one word about my fall came out of my mouth. Why? It's simple. That fall of mine that she and I both know she stole like a common thief was nothin' more than an object. It was somethin' that I could easily replace, and it had no sentimental value to it at all for me. Why, our friendship and the laughs we had were much more important then that stupid old fake hair could've ever been. So I never brought the topic up or questioned her friendship. After all, she must have needed it a lot more than I did. Of course, I did bring her in that next day two big batches of my special big chip chocolate chip cookies, which I make with love, care, and a box of Ex-Lax. I told her not to share 'em since I made 'em just for her. Whitney didn't make it back to class until the followin' Monday. She never said a word about the cookies, but bein' the good friends that we were, we both knew that the other had gotten the message. She moved a few years later to Seattle, and I lost contact with her. She was near and dear, and I'll never forget her. She sure could make a good pot of coffee.

And now, on to your letters.

Friends

Dear Ruby Ann,

My husband's best friend, Natty, insists on bringing his dog, Bullhorn, with him when he comes to visit. Bullhorn is an aging hunting dog. Now it ain't bad enough that he flips spit into my cooking when he shakes his head, but he also drools all over my brand-new linoleum, made to look like a wood floor. I've asked him not to bring Bullhorn with him to our home, but he and my husband say that where Natty goes Bullhorn goes. What should I do?

Signed,
Anguished in the Kitchen

Dear Anguished,

Cover your food with a lid and spot mop your floor a few extra times a day. My goodness, you call that a problem? If bendin' and heavy liftin' ain't involved, then it's not a problem but a small inconvenience. Just treat that dear old dog like you would if it was your grandma or grandpa stayin' over for a visit. Make sure it has a nice comfortable place to rest, fresh water to drink, and take it outside and hose it down after each meal.

> Love, Kisses, and Trailer Park Wishes,
> Ruby Ann Boxcar

Dear Ruby Ann,

I am a new bride of just six weeks. My parents gave me and my husband a new trailer for a weddin' present and right after our two-day honeymoon to Branson we moved in and have been so happy. My problem is my husband's friends. When we were datin' I never had to be around them very much, so we were always very pleasant around each other.

Now that we're married they want to come over to our trailer every night. All they want to do is drink, work on cars, and watch sports. Ruby Ann, if you hooked up jumper cables to all of them at once you wouldn't get a spark if you know what I mean. They have to be the dumbest, laziest pigs ever put on this earth. They're all too mean to live and too stupid to kill.

I don't want to hurt my husband's feelings, but they have got to go! We haven't spent one night alone since we got back from our honeymoon! My husband has not even wanted me in that "special way." When his friends leave every night around midnight, he's always a little bit drunk from all the beer, so he just rolls over and goes to sleep. What am I gonna do to get rid of these people? How can I turn my bedroom back into a happy honeymoon suite?

> Bewildered Bride

Dear BB,

This is one of the reasons that I say you should date for at least a week before gettin' married. But I guess it's a little too late to talk about that now. If you want your husband to pay more attention to you and less to his friends, then you've got to put a wedge between the two. You have to make your husband think twice about his friends. This can easily be done, and it will cost you very little. The one thing that will make a man mad is if he thinks his friends are hittin' on his wife. So what you have to do is entice these fellas into makin' sexual comments about you in front of your husband. Since they sound like real idiots, it should be easy. The first thing I'd do if I was you was to wait until the guys have had a few beers or whatever they might be drinkin'. Then walk out in front of the gang in a bathrobe, and ask your husband for advice. Tell him you just bought a new bathin' suit and want to know if you should take it back to the store or not. Before he can say anythin' else, drop the robe and show off the suit you have on underneath it. Now this should get some cat-calls or one of the boys will eventually say somethin' that they shouldn't when you leave. Just say yes to whatever your husband says to you about the suit. This should do the trick, and you will notice that both your bedroom experiences and the lack of nightly visits by your hus-band's friends will be where you want them to be. But before you try this, you might want to take my special "Public Swimsuit Wearin' Test," just to make sure that this is the right angle for you to take. Just answer the simple questions below after you've stepped outside on your front porch or lawn in your swimsuit.

1. Have the birds strangely gone silent?
2. Have any birds fallen from the sky?
3. Have all the dogs run off?
4. Did the weeds, plants, and flowers just die?
5. Are approachin' cars quickly turnin' around and drivin' the other way?
6. If you live next to water, has the beautiful babblin' brook stopped babblin'?
7. Have the neighbors closed their windows?
8. Are the Mormons by-passin' your house on bicycles at record-breakin' speeds?
9. When you stepped out the door, did you hear windows breakin'?
10. And last but not least, did an ambulance stop in your drive-way or in front of your home?

If you answered yes to any one of these questions, then you might want to skip the whole swimsuit thing and try to tempt your hus-band's friends with your cookin'. Just unbutton a few buttons on that blouse before bringin' out that cheesecake for the boys to enjoy.

Now, if you don't take my word and skip the warnin' about the bathin'suit thing, then at least carry a few cans or bottles of ice-cold beers out there with you. This will turn them boys on as much as if you was Raquel Welch or Tanya Tucker in the flesh.

Love, Kisses, and Trailer Park Wishes,
Ruby Ann Boxcar

Dear Ruby Ann,

How long do you have to wait before moving in on a friend's ex?

Miguel

Dear Miguel,

Your move and all depend on the closeness of your friendship. If y'all are best friends, then a month should be long enough to wait. If y'all are friends who do things together like fishin' and such, then two weeks. If y'all are drinkin' buddies who go out to the bars together, then twelve minutes should be long enough. Good luck.

Love, Kisses, and Trailer Park Wishes,
Ruby Ann Boxcar

Dear Ruby Ann Boxcar,

This year for my birthday, a close friend gave me a card and nothing else, which was fine. Now her birthday has come around and I don't know what to do. I want to give her a gift that I had already purchased for her last year and was waiting until now to give her, but I don't want to make her feel bad since she didn't give me anything for my birthday.

Signed,
Tammy C.

Dear Tammy,

Go ahead and just give her a card. She was most likely tryin' to tell you that she couldn't afford to give you a gift this year for whatever reason by simply givin' you that card. So most likely you would insult her. If you want to give that gift, wait for a few days and then go ahead and say that you found this and thought she might like it. Then it becomes a regular gift and not a birthday gift. If you are uncomfortable with that solution, then just wrap up the gift, put it in a box, and send it to me care of my publisher. I'm always glad to accept gifts.

Love, Kisses, and Trailer Park Wishes,
Ruby Ann Boxcar

Dear Ruby Ann,

I loaned my good suitcase out to a friend and the airline lost it. Now I have a trip coming up next month and need a suitcase. What should I do?

Signed,
Waiting to Pack

Dear Waiting,

I'd suggest you start savin' those plastic grocery bags. If you tie 'em by the handles, you can get a few shirts and a pair of pants in one. Momma and Daddy swear by their plastic luggage set.

As far as your friend goes, you really can't expect her to do anything until the airline decides that the luggage is lost for good. After that, it's a whole different story since the airlines by law have to give you up to $2,500 per bag if they can't locate the luggage that they lost. The one thing you can't expect right now is for your friend to go out and buy you a new suitcase, after all, she most likely can't afford it, which is why she asked to use yours in the first place. Good luck, and Momma says to make sure and double bag them plastic bags when packin' shoes.

Love, Kisses, and Trailer Park Wishes,
Ruby Ann Boxcar

And Enemies

Dear Ruby Ann,

Me and Darnell had been dating for twenty-three years, until an archenemy of mine went off and stole him from me. I could kill her, but I know that would be wrong. What should I do?

Signed,
Armed and Dangerous

Dear Dangerous,

You need to set right down and write that girl a thank-you card for takin' that bum off your hands. You do realize that nobody *dates* for twenty-three years, don't you? That ex of yours was kind of like that thing you got in your fridge with the foil on it. At one time it was real good, but now it just smells and needs to be tossed. I suggest that you take this as a sign from the good Lord above and move on.

Love, Kisses, and Trailer Park Wishes,
Ruby Ann Boxcar

Chapter 5

Social Events

My sister, Donna Sue, has come up with a new way of makin' extra money. Both kids and adults alike just love Bimbo the Clown.

*t*he way you behave and act at social gatherin's is so important, especially if you want to fit in or avoid an argument. As easy as that might sound, it ain't, and I got the questions to prove it. You see, things ain't always what they seem to be. For example, I was forty-three before I realized that all people didn't take their kids to Wal-Mart so they could spank 'em. You can imagine my shock. And who knew you couldn't talk to the actors at a play like you do to the ones on TV? Plus, nowadays we don't throw rice anymore at weddin's 'cause when birds eat it, it expands in their bellies and they die. Of course I'm now usin' that thing with the rice as my new excuse for my size. I mention all the above 'cause I got a feelin' that most of y'all already knew all about these things already. But what I've found was that y'all don't know jack when it comes to the correct and proper ways to behave at social events. Y'all are kind of like Hubert Bunch over in Lot #3 when he and his wife, Lois, attended a wine-tastin' event. After you taste the wine, you're supposed to spit it out in a bucket. Since there were only a few of us there, they had a fella who'd hold the bucket for you while you leaned over and spit into it. Well, not knowin' anything about this whole process, when the bucket came to him, Hubert threw change in it. He thought the fella wanted a tip. As you can guess Lois was so embarrassed. Mind you, her embarrassment didn't last for long. Let's just say that Lois and Blue Cheese don't get along, and we'll leave it at that.

And now for your letters.

105

Weddin's

Dear Ruby Ann,

How long should you wait before getting married? Is it a question of love or compromise?

Deep Thoughts,
Jamie Everret

Dear Jamie,

I say wait for love unless of course you happen to be dog-ugly like Opal Lamb, and in that case, get to that altar as fast as you can, before your groom or bride either sobers up or comes out of that coma.

Love, Kisses, and Trailer Park Wishes,
Ruby Ann Boxcar

Dear Ruby Ann,

If you're divorced, but you get an invitation from somebody in your ex's family about a graduation, wedding, or a birth announcement, do you have to send a gift?

M.H.

Dear M.H.,

I don't know why y'all are so evil sometimes! Of course you send a gift. If that person was kind enough to include you in that joyous celebration, then you should be kind enough to send a gift. The question you should be askin' is how much should your gift cost, and the answer to that is between $10 and $25. The correct thing to do is not to attend since this might cause some folks to feel uneasy, but instead to simply send your gift.

When it comes to shoppin' for your ex's family, I'd suggest that you send a subscription of *Playboy* and *Playgirl* to the happy wedding couple. A gift certificate for drinks at any local bar or strip club are always well received by a new high school graduate. And last but not least, a new Day-Timer with phone numbers for the doctor, hospital, Planned Parenthood, and orphanages already written in it makes for the perfect new baby present as well.

Love, Kisses, and Trailer Park Wishes,
Ruby Ann Boxcar

Dear Ruby Ann,

I am getting married and wonder where should I seat the pregnant girlfriend of my father?

Fluffie Pillows

Dear Fluffie,

Put her next to your mother's personal trainer.

Love, Kisses, and Trailer Park Wishes,
Ruby Ann Boxcar

Dear Ruby Ann,

My question is real simple. I am six months pregnant, and the father of my baby is not the man that I am marrying. The groom knows this, but he still insists that the soon-to-be baby's father takes part in the wedding. Ruby Ann, I don't know if I would feel comfortable with that, so I suggested that we just go out and get a different minister. What do you think?

Signed,
It's a Long, Long Story

Dear Long Story,

While you're at it, you might want to find a new church in a different state for that matter. Oh well, at least your new husband is either lovin' and understandin' or crazy as all get-out. Please tell me you ain't a Baptist!

Love, Kisses, and Trailer Park Wishes,
Ruby Ann Boxcar

Funerals

Dear Ruby Ann,

My best friend will be buried tomorrow. Will it be acceptable to wear my low-cut red dress with fishnet stockings if I stand in the back of the chapel? Her husband and I have a reservation at the Shady Lane Motel shortly after the services. I do not want to be late.

Signed,
Ima Hussy

Dear Hussy,

Well, of course you should wear that outfit; after all, if you wear anything else people will talk. And why stand around in the back? Come on down to the front pew if you want. Everybody knows you're nothin' more than two-dollar-turnin' gutter trash, so why try and dress like you ain't. Be proud of who you are, 'cause everybody else has already accepted you for the common slut that you happen to be. Dressin' down would be as stupid as me passin' up the dessert section at a buffet. People know I'm gonna have a piece of pie just like they know that you're about as easy as fryin' eggs in hell. Even the widower knows that you're a sure thing. After all, if he didn't, he would have left his wife for you a long time ago, wouldn't he? So put on those fishnets and dress like the cheap no-self-respect garbage that your dead friend and everyone in the community knows you to be. Have a nice day.

Love, Kisses, and Trailer Park Wishes,
Ruby Ann Boxcar

Dear Ruby Ann,

Lord knows I need your help. My grandpa of seventy-eight years of age has just passed away. In his last year on this earth he went a little crazy and made a written funeral request that the lawyer says is binding. He asked that the service be an open casket and that he be buried in my grandma's red negligee. As you can guess, Grandma is just beside herself and doesn't know what to do. She loves that red negligee and refuses to part with it. Do you think it would be OK if we just bury him in her chartreuse teddy instead, since it don't fit any-more and it does go better with the silver in his hair? I believe you'll know what's right.

Signed,
Troubled

Dear Troubled,

Let me start off by tellin' you how sorry I am for your loss. I've added your whole family to my prayer list. With that out of the way, I must say that I was appalled by your letter. I don't know what kind of people y'all are, but "normal" ain't the word for it. I thought some of the folks that I know were bad, but y'all take the cake. Chartreuse at a funeral? How tacky! I'd suggest you go with a little black lacy num-ber, accent it with a red boa, and be done with it. I'd also like to give y'all a suggestion on music if y'all don't mind. At the end of the ser-vice where they wheel your grandpa's casket down the aisle past all those in attendance, have the organist attempt a sassy version of the song "Big Spender." Now, that's class, plain and simple.

Love, Kisses, and Trailer Park Wishes,
Ruby Ann Boxcar

Dear Ruby Ann,

What is the deal with the elderly and funerals? It seems like every-one I know over the age of sixty-five spends more time at the funeral homes than they do at their own homes. Why is that?

Signed,
Wanting to Spend Time with Grandpa

Dear Wanting to Spend Time,

I think part of the reason is 'cause as they grow older, they have a lot more of friends and old co-workers or even folks from their church pass away. I'm sure for most of the seniors out there, the last thing they want to do is attend funerals, 'cause it usually means the loss of someone special in their lives. Of course that ain't true for all of 'em. My Me-Ma is a prime example of a different kind of attitude.

Every summer when Daddy and Momma would go on vacation or

a business trip, they'd leave me, my older sister, Donna Sue, and my even older brother, Jack Daniels, who has since gone on to meet his maker, with Me-Ma and Pa-Pa. Well, every night Me-Ma would scour the local paper for funerals in the surroundin' areas, and the next day while Pa-Pa and my brother were off workin', she'd dress me and Donna Sue up in our Sunday best, and haul us off to these funerals. We set there on those old benches and then head off to the reception with the rest of the mourners. Of course Me-Ma would cry and tell everyone how wonderful that deceased was, and how they will be sorely missed, as we filled our plates with food. She'd make us stuff our purses with bread items and cookies as well. Then we'd head out to the car and as we made our way to the next funeral, she'd have us dump our purses out into a big paper bag. That night at dinner, Me-Ma would serve a main dish along with our funeral bounty. The bad thing was that Me-Ma hadn't met one of these people when they was alive. All she knew about 'em was what she'd read in the paper. Now, as an adult, I finally realize the scars that the old woman and her funeral hoppin' have left on me. Why, even still today I can't pass a funeral home without gettin' hungry. And I wonder why I'm overweight.

> Love, Kisses, and Trailer Park Wishes,
> Ruby Ann Boxcar

Birthdays

Dear Ruby Ann,

My friend/boss has a birthday coming up soon (let's call her DSB). What could I possibly get for a woman that seems to have more than enough of everything. She likes to dance and drink. Help, I need ideas.

> F.D.

Dear F.D.,

Seein' how you give your boss gifts, I'm sure that with your magnificent taste, she already has all of my books as well as my sister, Donna Sue Boxcar's book, *Donna Sue's Down Home Trailer Park Bartending Guide.* Of course, bein' a good Baptist, I don't dance nor do I drink, at least not while I'm in town or while my trailer curtains are open. So I've had to pass this question on to my sister for her thoughts. She says that your boss sounds like the kind of person that might enjoy a board game, which I personally know I enjoy from time to time, especially Monopoly. Anyways, here are a few of the games that she suggests.

Sip 'N Go Naked by McNutty Games
Beer College by Paradogz Games
Spin the Bottle by McNutty Games
Sip 'N Strip by Passout Games
Wheel of Intoxication by Boingo Games
Pubcrawling by Northern Games
Chutes and Ladders by Hasbro

I hope this helps you with your gift-givin' dilemma.

Love, Kisses, and Trailer Park Wishes,
Ruby Ann Boxcar

Dear Ruby Ann,

My son is turning six very soon, so I want to throw him a special birthday party. He has made lots and lots of new friends during his first year in school, and I know he would love to have them over. I want this to be the best birthday party he has ever had. What do you suggest?

A Proud Mother

Dear Proud Mother,

I'd ask your friends who have children and see what they say. I know that clowns are real big at birthday parties. As a matter of fact, my sister, Donna Sue, rents herself out as a clown at afternoon birthday parties. The kids really love her, as do the parents. I don't know what her schedule is like, but if she ain't booked up, for just $25 and an open bar you, too, can have Bimbo the Clown at your next party. Not only does she do tricks like take her bra off without removin' her shirt and balancin' a vodka bottle on her knee while puttin' ice into a glass, but she also shapes balloons into body parts (you should see her ears and noses).

Love, Kisses, and Trailer Park Wishes,
Ruby Ann Boxcar

Anniversaries

Dearest Ruby Ann,

I have been married for the last thirty-four years and to this wife for the last four years. What is the five-year wedding anniversary? You know there is the silver one, the gold one, and so forth. I just need to know what to get her.

Eagerly Awaiting Your Answer,
Odell R. Sober

Dear Odell,

You must be a wonderful husband, rememberin' your weddin' anniversary and all. I know that there are several ladies at the High Chaparral Trailer Park where I live that would give their eyeteeth for their husbands to remember their anniversaries. Even my own daddy can't recall when him and Momma tied the knot. He blames it on Alzheimer's, which he ain't got. Of course Momma uses the same excuse when Daddy's ticked her off and she doesn't make dinner that night.

Nowadays, there are two lists, traditional and modern, when it comes to anniversary gifts. The traditional gift for five years of wedded bliss is wood, while the modern gift is silverware. I think I'd knock my husband back in time if he showed up on our anniversary with a box full of silverware. Go with the wood, but make it special like a grandfather clock or furniture. Just remember that the last thing you want to give her is a stick, a branch, or even a board, 'cause you might just get hit upside the head with it. Happy Anniversary to you both, and tell her I said, "Hi."

Love, Kisses, and Trailer Park Wishes,
Ruby Ann Boxcar

Dear Ruby Ann Boxcar,

Oh, I am mad! Today is my wedding anniversary and I just found out that my husband is cheating on me. My boyfriend said that he saw my husband sharing a cheese dog at the Sonic with some strange woman this afternoon. What should I do?

Signed,
Mad as a Hornet

Dear Hornet,

Suffer!

Love, Kisses, and Trailer Park Wishes,
Ruby Ann Boxcar

Births

Dear Ruby Ann,

My neighbor's sister's cousin, who I've met in the past, has given birth to Siamese twins. Does this mean I have to buy two gifts?

Signed,
Molly

Dear Molly,

I'm afraid so. But you might check into gettin' a quantity discount.

Love, Kisses, and Trailer Park Wishes,
Ruby Ann Boxcar

Dear Ruby Ann,

My sister in-law has had yet another baby for a grand total of twelve so far. I tell you, if she keeps this up, she's going to have more kids than roaches running around that trailer. My brother makes good money so he can afford to have that many kids, but his poor wife is about to drop. How can I tell him gracefully that he should think about usin' contraceptives? We're not Catholic, so he doesn't have a religious problem with using the stuff. Can you give me some suggestions to help my sister-in-law?

Signed,
A Loving Brother

Dear Loving Brother,

The first thing you can do is to volunteer at least once a week to come over and help her out with your nieces and nephews. I'm sure she'd love that. The next thing you can do is talk to your daddy and momma and pressure them to speak with your brother. If that don't work, then throw him in the car and make a road trip to the Blue Whale Strip Club where my sister dances. Trust me, regardless of how manly your brother might be, after viewin' a show there, the last thing to ever cross his mind will be sex.

> Love, Kisses, and Trailer Park Wishes,
> Ruby Ann Boxcar

Special Holidays

Dear Ruby Ann,

Do you have any suggestions for a rip-roarin' Groundhog Day celebration?

> Thanks,
> Michaela

Dear Michaela,

Groundhog Day is one of those few days in the year that you'll find us trailer folk gettin' up early in the mornin'. If we don't have to get up for work, then normally we sleep in at least until 8:30, but on Groundhog Day we rise with the sun. As you well know, typically around the country people celebrate Groundhog Day by usin' a groundhog, but here at the High Chaparral Trailer Park we do it a bit differently. There are two traditions that we practice when it comes to predictin' the return of spring. The first one is my favorite and it involves my stripper/professional drinker sister, Donna Sue. We gather up all the kids in the surroundin' area before they head off to school, and have 'em throw rocks at Donna Sue's trailer. If she comes cussin' out the back door of her trailer, then it's six more weeks of winter, but if she comes cussin' out the front trailer door, then spring arrives early. And if her one-night stand comes out either door, we call the police, 'cause more than likely there's goin' to be trouble.

The second tradition, which we started just four short years ago, takes place later in the day, around 4:00 P.M., so all the kids can enjoy it. What we do is dress my Me-Ma up in a groundhog costume and set her loose half a block from the trailer park. Now, if she makes it back in an hour, then it's six more months of winter. Of course the sheriff told us that what we was doin' to Me-Ma was considered inhumane, and that we'd have to put a trackin' device on her before settin' her free from now on. I must admit, that little trackin' thing came in real handy two years ago when a bear drug Me-Ma back to its cave, but I'm sure the police dogs would've found her eventually regardless.

Since this ain't a real big holiday, we really don't do much for it as far as decoratin', preparin', or activities go other than what I mentioned above. Because of this, we usually lay back down in the afternoon for a nap since we had to get up so dang early. I hope that helps!

Love, Kisses, and Trailer Park Wishes,
Ruby Ann Boxcar

Dear Ruby Ann,

My husband and I recently moved to Texas because of his work. While here I found out that they do several things different than we in the North do. Some of these new ways have been great, while others, well, are not so great. But one of the new celebrations that my husband and I recently stumbled upon is Guy Fawkes Day. What we found so amazing about this is was how it is a British holiday that has made it to Texas because of all the British citizens that live in the state. I searched through my copy of your holiday cookbook, but I couldn't find any reference to it in there. Have you heard about this before, and if so, will you please share a little background on it so my husband and I don't sound so stupid when we tell people about our newest holiday?

Gone Country Texas Style

Dear Gone Country,

Welcome to the South! And, yes, I do know all about Guy Fawkes Day, and as a matter of fact, I'd originally included it in my holiday

cookbook, but we had to take it out on account of space. As you
might know, it falls on November 5 each year. This English celebration began long ago after this fella named Guy Fawkes and some of
his buddies put thirty-six barrels of gunpowder in a basement under
Parliament, which is kind of like our Capitol in Washington, D.C.
Anyways, their plan was to blow up the Parliament and the king on
November 5, but after an anonymous tip, old Fawkes was found with
the matches in his pocket. The king was saved, and Guy Fawkes and
the others involved were tortured and executed. So every year on
what has become known as Guy Fawkes Day or Bonfire Day, all
good Brits and even some Americans who like to have a good time
begin the celebratin'. Actually the whole thing starts on the fourth of
November by playin' practical jokes on people, but the real fun begins on the fifth with the Guy Fawkes effigy, the bonfire, and fireworks.

Now, traditionally kids make an effigy of Guy Fawkes, which, before they burn it at the bonfire, is carried around while the little kids
ask folks to give 'em a "Penny for the Guy?" The people then give
the kids a penny, which the kids keep. Well, at the High Chaparral
we changed that tradition just a bit. Since we don't really have any
kids other than Harlinda and Bonita Hix, we decided that each year
we'd just pick a trailer family to do the Guy Fawkes doll. So the first
year went to Harland and his family since they did have kids. They
made the Guy Fawkes doll out of an old scarecrow that they'd saved
from Halloween, put it on two poles, and carried it from the entrance
of the park to the office while sayin' "Penny for the Guy?" Well, rather
than just givin' 'em a penny, everybody started viciously slingin'
handfuls of change at 'em. I'm tellin' y'all it was just hateful! By the
time they got that doll to the office, they'd been hit with a good thirty
dollars in coins. Of course Harland went back and picked up the
change, but the whole Hix household had little welts on their bodies
for days to come. When me and my husband Dew's turn came up the
next year, we put on three layers of clothin', steel-toed boots, thick
work gloves, and welders' hats to protect ourselves, but it wasn't
enough. I swear to the good Lord above, there must not have been a
single doggone coin left in the Pangburn National Bank that day. I'm
tellin' you, it was bad, and even though we were all dressed up in protective gear, some of those coins found their mark. Folks, you don't
know what pain truly is till you've been hit upside the head with a
flyin' Kennedy half dollar! But me and my husband, Dew, didn't complain, we just walked faster. And when all was said and done, we'd

collected $328 in change, $6.26 in Canadian money, two pesos, four tokens, and a marble (if I ever find out who threw that dang marble, he's gonna regret that he was ever born). Well, me and my husband, Dew, put that money in the bank and the next year on Guy Fawkes Day, before the walkin' of the Guy, we took it and the interest it had acquired out in Eisenhower dollars. You see, you don't mess with lot #18 and live to tell about it.

I hope that helped to shed a little light on it for you and your hubby. Now, I also know that a lot of drinkin' can be involved with the whole holiday as well, so here is a warnin' to you just in case you, like myself, happen to live in a trailer park. Fireworks operated by drunks don't mix with trailer homes! Other than that, have a good time.

Love, Kisses, and Trailer Park Wishes,
Ruby Ann Boxcar

Public Pools

Dear Ruby Ann Darling,

My friends have all decided to have a get-together at their apartments' swimming pool. They have rented the whole thing out so only their good friends and their good friends' guests will be allowed to use the pool. I love my friends, and really want to go, but I don't have the best body. Should I forget about that part and simply go to have fun regardless of what others might say, or should I give some lame excuse and spend the afternoon locked inside my house filled with shame?

Signed,
Funnier Than Flipper

Dear Funnier,

Forget what people say, and just go enjoy yourself. After all, what's the worst that can happen? So what if a few people get sick in the pool when you take your robe off. That is their own fault. You need to have the same type of attitude my daddy recently had when we all went to Vegas. He knew he didn't have a great body, and that he was extremely overweight, but he was bound and determined to get in that hotel pool. So he quickly took off his bad toupee, disrobed, and dove in before anyone could see him. He swam around for a while in the deep end and then finally made his way to the shallow area so he could order a drink from the cocktail waitress. He kept hollerin', "Excuse me, miss," but with all the noise and such she couldn't hear him. So my father stood up in the shallow pool and started to reach out and flag her down as she walked by in order to get her attention. Well, before he could say a word, the lifeguard blew his whistle from his perch above the pool, pointed at my father, and then yelled out, "Pardon me, madam, but you've lost your top." As you can guess, Daddy just slid back into the water, forgetting about his thirst, and then made his way back over to the deep end, where he tried to hide behind Momma as she floated aimlessly on her heavy-duty raft. I guess the moral is that Daddy, who could've simply just not gotten into the swimmin' pool in the first place, or just got out right after the incident and in total embarrassment with his rather large man breasts swingin' in the wind, grabbed his hairpiece, towel, and robe, and went and hid in his hotel room, enjoyed the pool just like all the other payin' guests, without worry of what others thought. And that made me proud of Daddy. I learnt that life is full of fun, but too many of us are just too afraid to stop and enjoy it on account of what others might say. So you get that swimsuit and you go have a good time with your friends. Don't let them spoil your good time. Be like my daddy, and learn the lesson that he learnt that day. Well, actually there were two lessons he learnt. Number one, enjoy life, period, and number two, unless you like havin' people point at you and giggle for the rest of your stay, gamble in a different casino than the one you swim at.

Love, Kisses, and Trailer Park Wishes,
Ruby Ann Boxcar

Dearest Ruby Ann,

I am writin' you about public pool etiquette. I need to know a polite way to tell someone that she is not welcome to come back to our community pool as long as she is wearin' what is called a Brazilian T-back bikini. I don't know if you have ever seen one. I am not sure if I have seen the whole thing to be honest, but I have seen at least part of one. You see, Leanna Kay Burkett is a rather large woman who comes to the pool wearin' this bikini thing. I am surprised she can find it again to take it back off. I don't mean to be rude, but it is just wrong, wrong, wrong! Now she is a pretty girl in the face, and when she is wearin' clothes, but I mean to tell you this is not appropriate attire for a public pool. There are kids around that see this. Please tell me a way to let her know that this is not appropriate attire without hurting her feelings or embarrassing her.

Swimmin' with Whales

Dear Swimmin',

I must tell you that I found your letter to be horrific. What right do you have to say that a person can or cannot swim in the public pool? After all, this is not *your* pool, but rather it is the pool for the *public* to use, and since this Leanna Kay Burkett is part of the public, then she can swim wearin' anything she wants to any doggone day of the week. So what if she ain't the most attractive thing in the world or her swimsuit choices are almost unbearable? Lord knows we're always seein' parts of Jennifer Lopez and Pamela Anderson in every magazine we pick up. Why, you wouldn't think Christina Aguilera would know how to fasten a button or zip up a zipper with all the flesh she's throwin' around ever time you see one of her videos. Leanna Kay Burkett is just as free as these gals to let everybody see what the good Lord and them snack cake companies gave her. And it might even allow the little boys in the pool to see that it's OK to find a big woman attractive and give the little girls an early lesson on the horrors of stretch marks. Until the city council outlaws the use of these Brazilian T-backs at the public pool, all you can do is grin and bear it or go get yourself a turtle pool and enjoy it at home. I'm sorry if I seem a little mad or irate about this whole thing, but just last summer we had an incident that was similar to this take place at the High Chaparral Trailer Park.

Little Linda in Lot #20 would invite her friend Flora Delight, who as y'all know is temporarily livin' in Lot #19, and my sister, Donna Sue, from Lot #6 over to help her with her gardenin' and yard care. Then they'd go over to my sister's trailer and work on her yard. Since all three of these gals are exotic dancers by night, the idea that these rather large women throwin' on a two piece to do their outdoor lawn care might offend somebody didn't even cross their minds. Well, several neighbors did complain to Ben Beaver about the whole thing, and so now the policy at the High Chaparral Trailer Park states that we can't do yard work in anything less than a halter top and cutoff jeans. This policy just ticked me off 'cause even though the lots we live in do actually belong to the trailer park, that little area that we rent should be our private world, and as long as these gals ain't breakin' any laws, then they should be able to wear what they want. I don't know if this whole thing makes me mad 'cause of the political ramifications or simply 'cause since these gals have had to wear more clothin' when they work in the yard, the mice problem I had in my trailer has returned. Needless to say, as a member of the trailer park board, I'm doin' my darndest to get this new policy changed. After all, I can't afford to keep buyin' traps every doggone week.

So basically what I'm tryin' to say is shut up and let this gal enjoy all the aspects of life.

Love, Kisses, and Trailer Park Wishes,
Ruby Ann Boxcar

Bingo

Dear Ruby Ann,

I need your help. I think I have become an addict. I can't function anymore as a wife or mother. I don't want my husband to touch me. I don't care about my house or the bill collectors knockin' at my door. My poor kids are always next door at my mother's because they can't stand to be around me. I need help. Do you know if there is a Twelve Step program for bingo?

Dysfunctional Dauberer

Dear Dysfunctional,

You are not alone! My Me-Ma has this same problem with bingo, which, when you consider that they play it every night at the Last Stop Nursing Home where she lives, is an everyday battle for her. Well, luckily we were able to get her help, but first, as you well know, she had to see the problem. This head doctor that we got her worked wonders. He was able to get her off her bingo addiction in just days. He told her that she needed to make a list of things that she enjoys like food or old movies or music, and when she starts feelin' like she has to play bingo to do one of these other things instead. Needless to say, she ain't played bingo in over two weeks. Of course the nursin' staff have had to keep draggin' her out of the rooms of some of them bedridden male residents at the Last Stop Nursing Home for that amount of time as well, but she ain't had a dauber in her hand in two weeks.

Love, Kisses, and Trailer Park Wishes,
Ruby Ann Boxcar

Sports

Dear Ruby Ann,

The other night while playing poker with some friends, I noticed the most unseemly and permeating odor comin' off of one of the fellas. We played until everyone almost passed out from the odor. . . . My question? Do you think we should have said something to the offending player or do you think this was his winning strategy, seeing as how we all played like crap after that because our eyes were watering from the stench?

No Nose for Poker

Dear No Nose,

Since this fella with the stench won money, you really do have a problem, 'cause he will be back to try and win more. As I see it, you've only got five choices in this matter.

1. Send out invites to the next poker party that read "Since the playin' will be hot and heavy, make sure to bathe and put on lots of deodorant before comin' over for cards."

2. Accidentally spill a bottle of pancake syrup all over him while he's seated. Apologize and then show him to the bathroom to bathe. While his clothes are washin', let him wear a robe or such. Just remember to point out the soap and deodorant often before and even after he bathes.

3. Pull him aside before the next game day and tell him that somebody smelled really bad at that last game so if it happens again, you're gonna have to ask that person to leave.

4. Tell him the truth.

5. Just don't invite his stinky unwashed nasty smellin' self over.

> Love, Kisses, and Trailer Park Wishes,
> Ruby Ann Boxcar

Dear Ruby Ann,

My brother is a big fat cheat and I don't know what to do about it. He weighs close to four hundred pounds and when we play any kind of game, he uses his bulk to his advantage. It doesn't matter if it's cards, Monopoly, or whatever; he hides things under his legs, his stomach, and even his arms. What can I do to make him stop?

> Signed,
> Mad Sister

Dear Mad,

This is an easy one. Next time y'all play a game, seat your brother in an old rickety chair. I guarantee that sometime durin' the game that chair of his will give out, and he will go crashin' to the floor with the hidden cards or other items layin' around him on the floor. Then you have him dead to rights. You've caught him cheatin' plain and simple, and there is nothin' he can say to get out of it. Just make sure you don't have any valuable items settin' around him, or even a wall for that matter.

> Love, Kisses, and Trailer Park Wishes,
> Ruby Ann Boxcar

Las Vegas

Dear Ruby Ann,

This e-mail is from two Baptists to another, and even though we don't have the same kind of secrecy the Catholics do in the confessional, I know that you will keep this between the three of us. Our church choir has been invited to perform a concert at a rather posh Baptist church in Las Vegas next month, and our choirmaster accepted the gracious offer. Our problem is that we've never been to Las Vegas, and being more on the liberal side of the faith, we want to do a little gambling as well. But I'm afraid one of the other choir members might see us. I know from your last book that you've been to Vegas and have also gambled there. Would you please give us a few ideas as to what we should do if this situation does crop up? Thank you, and God Bless.

Ken and Elaine Arnett
Springfield, Missouri

Dear Ken and Elaine,

You're right, we Baptists don't have the secrecy of the confessional, and since your problem deals with an issue that would best be helped by understandin' and prayer, I'm gonna let everyone know what your situation is so that when they pray, they know what they're prayin' about. In this case, they'd be prayin' that nobody sees y'all's behinds in the Rio!

Yes, Ken and Elaine, y'all are right about my dabblin's in gamblin'. I do enjoy pullin' a few slot machine handles or playin' a bit of black jack or three-card poker from time to time, and for a while I was just like y'all, worried that someone might see me. But my fears all went away when Pastor Ida May Bee preached on the topic of gamblin' just this past year. You see, the church ladies were torn between spendin' our yearly weekend vacation in either Branson, Missouri, or Shreveport, Louisiana. Well, as you might have guessed, Sister Bertha wanted to go to Branson to see Tony Orlando and Pastor Ida May Bee wanted to go to Shreveport to gamble. Sister Bertha kept talkin' about how with all that gamblin' goin' on, Shreveport would be nothin' but a den of sin. So on the Sunday before the vote, Pastor Ida May Bee got up and said that nowhere in the Bible does it say that gamblin' is a sin.

"Brothers and especially sisters," Pastor Ida May preached, "in the first book of Timothy it says that 'The love of money is the root of all evil.' Well, if any of y'all have ever set down at one of them red, white, and blue or even wild cherry slot machines, you well know that you can't love your money and play that game for very long, 'cause most of the time you're gonna kiss them nickels, dimes, and freshly rolled quarters good-bye.

Some out there in this church would say that gamblin' is inconsistent with a Christian lifestyle, which includes providin' for one's own family and givin' to those in need. To them I say, if you've ever seen the way Sister Ruby Ann can tear up one of those Las Vegas buffets, you'd know the little bit of money that I lose on keno goes to help those casino owners in need after she's pushed away from the table.

And even others would have you believe that by gamblin' you're betrayin' the idea that God will provide. That can also be said about fillin' out that application for a job promotion as well. The idea of just settin' back until God gets your boss to walk up to you and say, "Hey, Brother So and So, or Sister So and So, God told me to give you more money," is about as dumb as sayin' that dear old Brother Riley settin' right up here in the front pew wasn't a good Baptist since he worked the same low-rung job position for twenty-nine years. All that means is that Brother Riley wasn't very good at what he did and made a real bad career choice. By the way, Brother Riley, while you're out there in the vestibule, would you get me a little glass of water, please. Thank you, Brother.

So in conclusion, if you spend no more on gamblin' than you would at a night down at the Dusty Comet Auto Park Drive-in with admission, snacks, and refreshments, the gas that you use to run your car so you can defog your windshield every five minutes, and the cost of the Shout to get that mystery butter substance that they put on their popcorn out of your good double knit polyester slacks, then all you've done is enjoy another form of entertainment. So as long as you play responsibly and, if you're at the black jack table I'm playin' at, accordin' to the basic rules of game play, then I say God bless you.

Needless to say, we ladies went to Shreveport.

Now, on to what to do if somebody sees you in a casino. The first thing you want to do is act natural, as if you weren't doin' anything. Then relax, and follow these instructions. There are a few things that a good Baptist can say, and each one depends on where they see you. So I'll quickly break it up for you by namin' the location in the casino, what to do, and then what to say.

- **Caught at a card table:**
  While noddin' towards the dealer, quietly say, "Just thirty more minutes and I'll have converted another Methodist."

- **Caught at a slot machine:**
  Look at the money tray on the slot and loudly ask, "Don't tell me my Butterfinger is stuck in this doggone thing!"
- **Caught at the craps table:**
  Point towards the stickman and say, "This fella's got the server, so I'm sure the pizzas should be out any second now."
- **Caught at the bar in the lounge:**
  Regardless of what kind of drink you are holdin', take a drink and say, "Why, this ain't apple juice." (This even works with umbrella-accented frozen drinks.)
- **Caught at the roulette table:**
  Look at the croupier and loudly exclaim, "Pat, I'd like to buy a vowel."
- **Caught in the keno lounge:**
  Simply sigh, then say, "Oh my feet."

Hopefully these small suggestions will help y'all to have a good-clean-fun time. Oh, and remember what I always say, regardless of what others might tell you or imply, tippin' the waitress, waiter, cock-tail waitress, or bartender with religious tracts instead of money is not a form of Christian love or compassion. So have a great time and sing real good.

Love, Kisses, and Trailer Park Wishes,
Ruby Ann Boxcar

Chapter 6

School

A star was born—thanks to the talented ear of my then music teacher and now neighbor over in Lot #4, Nellie Tinkle. Boy, were we young.

With Nellie Tinkle livin' over in Lot #4, every day I see her I'm reminded of my youth. After all, as most of y'all will recall me sayin' in my first book, dear old Ms. Tinkle was my music teacher in school. She had me from first grade all the way up until I graduated. As a matter of fact, to this day when someone asks, after someone has heard my singin' abilities onstage, "Who told you that you could sing," I'm always proud to say Nellie Tinkle. She took this naturally gifted musical voice of mine and handcrafted it durin' those school years to make me into the temptress of song that I am today. Of course, that might just be one of the reasons that I loved school. I mean, my late older brother was much better at after-school sports than I ever was, and believe it or not, my sister brought home nothin' but straight A's all the way up until the day she graduated. So naturally, since I was the youngest one in the family, teachers compared me to them every day of the school year from kindergarten up to my senior year. And as you can guess, my grade card wasn't ever full of A's or even B's for that matter, but I could sing like a doggone angel. That is one of the reasons that I believe when the good Lord gives you a little in this area he makes up by blessin' you with a lot in another area. Although my niece, Lulu Bell, is the exception to that rule. But, as I said, not a day goes by that I don't think of me standin' by that piano liftin' my voice in song as my musical teacher, Nellie Tinkle, lovingly looks at me with pride while she tries to play the piano, turn the sheet music, and ash her cigarette all at the same time. She gave up her chain-smokin' ways back in 1972 after the school that I attended mysteriously burnt to the ground.

And now for your letters.

First Day of School

Dear Ruby Ann,

My little one is just scared to death about his first day of school. What can I tell him to make him calm down?

A Worried Mom

Dear Worried Mom,

Just tell him that there will be monkeys there. Every child likes monkeys, so he will be happy to attend his first day of school. Of course he'll never trust you again and look like a stupid idiot 'cause he'll keep askin' the teacher where the monkeys are, but at least he'll do all this at school.

Love, Kisses, and Trailer Park Wishes,
Ruby Ann Boxcar

School Lunches

Dear Ruby Ann,

Should I make my daughter's lunches when she starts school or should I just give her money for the school lunch?

Greta

Dear Greta,

I know you ain't gonna get up early enough to make your daughter's lunch every school day, and there ain't nothin' worse than a soggy sandwich that's set in the bag overnight in the fridge. Besides, if it weren't for school lunches, how would we ever have known that corn went so well with sloppy Joes or pizza? Pay for the doggone lunches. Plus there are elderly women who rely on you to keep them employed in the cafeteria. The last thing you want is them loose on the streets durin' the day or drivin' on the roads in the afternoons.

Love, Kisses, and Trailer Park Wishes,
Ruby Ann Boxcar

Parent-Teacher Day

Dear Ruby Ann,

Who in the world invented Parent–Teacher Day at the school? We have to take off work and miss out on valuable pay to go to the school and talk to the teacher about our children's grades and behavior.

It's bad enough I have to go two or three times a week to visit the principal's office and to the darn probation officers but why do I have to go see some uppity old battleax about my kids' grades? All they ever tell me is that my kids won't ever amount to anything. I could have told them that the day they were born! Is there any way to get out of going? Is there a petition of some kind I can sign or maybe could we take it to a vote?

Emma Jean Watson of Birmingham

Dear Emma Jean,

No I'm sorry, there is no petition to sign or ballot to vote on in regards to Parent–Teacher Day. I'm afraid that just like your parents, you and your kids, when they grow up, too, will have to keep attendin' these school functions to find out just how backward your children really are, until someone in your family catches on and has her tubes tied.

Love, Kisses, and Trailer Park Wishes,
Ruby Ann Boxcar

Homework

Dear Ruby Ann,

What's up with teachers these days? My kids come home from school nearly every day with homework. What are they doin' at school all day that they can't get it done there? Are these teachers takin' two-hour lunches and watchin' soap operas in the teachers' lounge?

I nursed them kids, diapered 'em (pretty near fillin' up one whole landfill with Huggies), waitin' for the day they'd start school, and the teacher sends 'em home with homework? I did my nine years in school and got married like Momma told me too.

I shouldn't have to know the capital of Norway; I'm a mom just tryin' to make a happy trailer park home for my family. Why would my kids need to know the square root of anything? They need to know how to get the electric company to let your power stay on for three more days till your husband gets the money from his momma's life insurance. Who was the first person to sign the Declaration of Independence? Who cares—what's more important is who does the hirin' at the Piggly Wiggly and when are they takin' applications for bag boys? How is our country gonna help some foreign country get back on its feet? It's more like how to feed a family of seven with $10 left in food stamps—now those are questions I can answer!

What can I do to get that teacher to get off her butt and make them do that work at school? I have better things to do.

Housewife Homework 101

Dear 101,

You're preachin' to the choir, sister. Thank the good Lord above my dogs don't have to go to school, or I'd be up the creek without a paddle, if you know what I mean.

By the way, the capital of Norway is Oslo. The only reason I know that is 'cause Opal Lamb dated a man for a year that soon after their breakup went to Oslo and had one of them sex changes. Opal always has had a way of changin' people in one way or another.

Love, Kisses, and Trailer Park Wishes,
Ruby Ann Boxcar

Prom

Dear Ruby Ann,

Last weekend my boyfriend went to juvenile detention, and now I'm without a date for the prom. It's only two weeks away and I may be the only gal left in town that doesn't have a date! My cousin offered to take me and so did my stepdad (who is considerably younger than my mom, by the way). But I want to keep my options open. What do you think?

No Chance for Prom Queen

Dear No Chance,

Personally I've always been a "stand by your man" kind of gal, which means that if I was you, I'd just go alone or stay at home since my man was incarcerated, but again that's just me. So what I did was I went to the source on datin' men behind bars at the High Chaparral Trailer Park, which of course is Little Linda. Accordin' to this felon-lovin' neighbor, you should still go to the prom, but go by yourself. Even though your man is incarcerated, the love he feels for you is still just as strong today as it was before he wore handcuffs. So respect him enough to go without a date. Not only does this show him that you feel the same way too, but Little Linda says that it also allows you to mess around with all the other guys at the prom without bein' chained down to just the fella that brung you.

Love, Kisses, and Trailer Park Wishes,
Ruby Ann Boxcar

Reunions

Dear Ruby Ann,

I have a high school reunion coming up and I'd like to look my best. Do you have any suggestions for losing a few pounds?

Sally

Dear Sally,

As you might have guessed, I'm not the queen of weight loss. Mind you, I have tried. My niece, Lulu Bell, got me that Jane Fonda workout tape one year and I lost forty pounds. I went into a coma durin' the first five minutes and they didn't find me for two weeks. Then there was the time I took up walkin' down my road. That did work. The police pulled me over, they thought I was a stolen van. And then I tried that rowin' machine. Well, it came off the tracks and I was halfway to Dallas before it stopped.

Currently I've gotten hooked on the local gym over by where I live. They got one of them motorized treadmills that you can walk on regardless of the weather. You tell it how fast you want to go, and it turns that belt at that speed, which helps to assure that you don't keep stoppin' or slowin' down. I still eat what I want, and then every day I go walk a mile to a mile and a half on that treadmill. I tell you, in just two weeks I've lost eight pounds and only burnt up three motors. Good luck to you.

Love, Kisses, and Trailer Park Wishes,
Ruby Ann Boxcar

Chapter 7

Church

Most likely this will be the last year for the gun show at the church on account of how somebody accidentally discharged and shot out the baptismal tank.

*Y*ou know, dear reader, church is very important to us trailer park folks for the simple reason that it gives us hope that regardless of how many times we might be out of work, late on our bills, or on *COPS*, there will eventually be a better life. It also helps to remind us that we are loved, and I ain't talkin' about the kind of love a parent has for a child, a spouse has for a partner, or a cousin has for another cousin, but a love that is always and is forever unconditional. This love and faith of ours allows us to handle any burden, overcome any obstacle, and forgive any wrongdoing. (Of course most of us are still workin' on that last one.) It also gives us a place where we can feel that we belong, regardless of what Sister Bertha and her haggard group of supporters might tell you otherwise. 'Cause when we're in church, we're in God's house, and we are one big family who gather together and share our lives. Some folks from time to time tend to share a bit more of their lives than you actually wanted or even cared to know about. But that's OK in church.

Church also allows us to become a close-knit society that shares its food with one another. In the Baptist church, there are two requirements that all members must meet. They must be baptized and they must know how to make a good casserole or side dish. Even though the second requirement ain't actually mentioned durin' an altar call, it is somethin' that's expected from you, regardless of your past religious affiliations, at your first church potluck.

Even if there wasn't a heaven or even an afterlife of any kind, the potluck would still be reason enough to be a Baptist. Once a month at the Holier Than Most Baptist Church we have a potluck that would put any restaurant to shame. I know that might be hard for you non-Baptists who've eaten at a Golden Corral, Sizzler, or Red Lobster to believe, but it's true. There is a spread of every side dish, dessert, and casserole that you can imagine, and they're all loaded with taste. They're also loaded with calories, but Pastor Ida May Bee assures us that her prayer over the food takes care of all them.

And just like with any family, you're gonna have your problems, which as you will see, are many. Some of these situations are big while others are real small. Some are due to others in the church and some are on not knowin' what to do in church. But regardless of what they might be, they're still problems that can easily be solved, 'cause as long as the good Lord is in his heaven, then there is always a good time to be had in his house. With that said, the one thing that I find funny about the letters I get is that folks are comin' to me rather than their pastors with these problems. Maybe if the Lord hadn't seen fit to give me such a beautiful singin' voice and a special way with makeup and hair, I might have found my way behind the pulpit at the Holier Than Most Baptist Church. Of course if that had been the case, we'd have had potluck more often than once a month, I can tell you that.

And now for your letters.

Potluck

Dear Ruby Ann,

OK, I need you to end an argument. What is the difference be-tween a casserole and a hot dish? I'm from the North originally, and I don't know what to take to the potluck we are having at church on Sunday. And yes, I am a Baptist. I was raised Lutheran, but to my mother's horror, I married into the Baptist faith. So please help me.

Thank you,
Inga S.

Dear Inga,

I know that this can be a problem for not only you former Lutherans, but also for all you Northerners as well. It really is simple. In the trailer park as well as in the South, a casserole is somethin' that you bake *in* the stove, and a hot dish is somethin' you bake *on* the stove. And regardless of what you've heard, a real-life casserole has got to spend some kind of time cookin' in the stove. I know that there are some folks out there who will layer a dish and put it in a Crock-Pot, and call it a casserole. Well, not only is that not right, it's just plain out unnatural. Now if you were to take that mixture and put it in a casserole dish and pop it in a hot oven for an additional five minutes, then you might have a casserole. But if not, then that, too, would simply be a hot dish. Now I also know that someone out there who lives in a trailer park or even in the South is gonna disagree with me, but that just goes to prove Sister Bertha's point that the Lutherans are infiltratin' at record speeds.

Love, Kisses, and Trailer Park Wishes,
Ruby Ann Boxcar

Dear Ms. Boxcar,

We are having a potluck at my church this next weekend in honor of two missionaries. They are from China, so I wanted to bring a special Asian dish that no one else would bring. I thought that would keep with the theme of the slide show they will be presenting after the potluck. Do you have any ideas?

Bonnie Tucker

Dear Bonnie,

I think that sounds like a wonderful idea of makin' an Oriental dish for these soldiers of the Lord. We did somethin' like that a few years back for some Ethiopian missionaries that put on a presentation at our church. All of us ladies decided we'd do an Ethiopian dish for our potluck. We ended up with thirty-seven rice casseroles and a bakin' dish full of sand. My niece, Lulu Bell, brung the sand. God bless her, she ain't all there.

Anyways, since I don't know what kind of budget you're on, I'm includin' two of my favorite Chinese dishes. I'm sure that regardless of which one you select to make, you'll still be the talk of the church function.

Shanghai Beef Baloney

*This dish will make your missionaries feel like they was
back in China.*

Makes 4 to 6 servin's

> 2 tablespoons oil
> 1 pound beef baloney
> 8-ounce can sliced water chestnuts, drained
> 1 red capsicum, sliced
> 5 scallions, cut into strips
> ½ teaspoon salt
> ¼ teaspoon black pepper
> 1 can condensed beef broth
> ¼ cup water
> 4 tablespoons soy sauce
> 2 tablespoons cornstarch
> 1½ cups dry rice

Get the oil hot in a skillet and fry the baloney for 2 minutes on each side.
Add the water chestnuts, capsicum, scallions, salt, and pepper. Stir it up and
cook for an additional 4 minutes.

Stir together the broth, water, soy sauce, and cornstarch. Mix well. Add
it to the mixture above. Keep cookin' until the mixture gets to a full boil (stir-
rin' occasionally). Add the rice and stir. When the rice gets soft, take it off
the heat and let it stand for around 5 minutes or so. Serve warm.

—WANDA KAY LOT #13

Fried Velveeta and Spam-Stuffed Wontons

If all Chinese food was this good, I'd eat it more often.

Makes 4 servin's

¼ pound Spam, cut into tiny little cubes
16 wonton skins
¼ pound Velveeta, cut into small cubes
Vegetable oil

Put a few pieces of Spam in the middle of each wonton skin. Next, put a few cubes of Velveeta in the middle of each and wrap the skins around the Spam and cheese. Twist to seal the sides. Heat the oil to 400 degrees F. and fry the wontons. Take 'em out when they've gotten nice and golden.

—LITTLE LINDA, LOT #20

Good luck with the potluck!

Love, Kisses, and Trailer Park Wishes,
Ruby Ann Boxcar

Dear Ruby Ann,

Why does potato salad always taste better when it was made in a church kitchen?

Wanita

Dear Wanita,

I'm afraid that after the last fire, we no longer are allowed to cook in the church kitchen except for the annual pancake breakfast that we do. So I don't even remember how church-cooked food tastes. I can tell you, though, that there ain't nothin' like the food that comes out of a Baptist's kitchen, that's for sure. We got more good-tastin' food recipes than Methodists got hand bells, Jehovah Witnesses got publications, Catholics got bingo cards, Russian Orthodox got icons, Mormons got wives, or Episcopalians got liquor bottles.

Now, I can give you a little hint as to how you can make some of your dishes taste more like the ones you've had at church functions. One word: paprika!

Love, Kisses, and Trailer Park Wishes,
Ruby Ann Boxcar

Offerin'

Dear Ruby Ann,

I need your advice. I don't go to church as often as I should, but I still consider myself a good Baptist girl. My daughter is always after me to attend more often, but in my profession it's hard to get up on Sunday mornings. Whenever I do go to church I never know how much to put in the offerin' plate. I know it is customary to give 10 percent of your income, and most of my money comes from tips on-stage, but do I include the income from lap dances too? And what about the money that I make from my psychic abilities? Should I put some of that money in the plate even though Sister Bertha says that it and my horoscope makin' are the work of the devil? Mind you, I think it's all talents from God myself, and to be honest I really don't listen to a word Sister Bertha says. After all, I've seen her wear white after Labor Day, so a lot she knows about nothin'.

Faye Faye LaRue

Dear Faye Faye,

If it was me, I'd personally go to the pastor and talk to them about it. I got a sneaky feelin' that your church is gonna be happy to take any money you want to put in that offerin' plate.

As far as Sister Bertha goes, don't pay her no mind. After all, the only thing she's an expert on is bitterness.

Love, Kisses, and Trailer Park Wishes,
Ruby Ann Boxcar

Baptism

Dear Ruby Ann,

I'm twenty-four years old and finally getting baptized by submersion, of course, at the new church that I recently joined. I'm very excited, but I don't know what to wear. And since I don't want to look like an idiot, I hate to ask anyone at the church. I can tell you that they give us these white robes to wear, but they said we need to wear something under the robe since you can kind of see through it when it gets wet. Do you think it would be all right to just wear my two-piece swimsuit? Of course I would wear an old Marilyn Manson T-shirt as well so not to offend anyone with my bare midriff.

Natasha

Dear Natasha,

Now, I don't know how old you are, but I can tell you that if you are over the age of fourteen and a size two or bigger, that wet white robe is gonna make your hips look like floatation devices. I'd stick with the swimsuit and the Marilyn Manson T-shirt, but I'd get some long black shorts to wear under it too. I'm assumin' that the T-shirt is black as well, since both the black shorts and shirt will give you a slender appearance under the white robe. If you ain't got black, then go with a dark brown or even blue, but stay away from white unless you want to come up from the water surrounded by whale-fishin' boats, and red is terrible 'cause it'll run, turnin' that white baptismal robe into a lovely pink frock. Good luck and hold your nose.

Love, Kisses, and Trailer Park Wishes,
Ruby Ann Boxcar

Bad Singin'

Dear Ruby Ann,

We have a dear sweet elderly lady at church, who thinks she is an opera star when it comes to singing—her voice has scared most of the children and has caused several hearing aids to blow. She is a sweet old soul, so no one wants to hurt her feelings, but aspirin can only do so much (as can cotton in the ears). One suggestion from a congregation member was to seat her next to the missionaries that have just gotten back from Toronto and tell her not to open her mouth too wide or breathe too much cause you never know if they have been in contact with that SARS stuff. I have to admit that I've never had bad thoughts about anybody, but the past few Sundays I've actually thought about praying that she gets monkey pox. Any other suggestions?

Thanks,
Sunday Afternoon with a Headache

Dear Headache,

Have y'all talked to your pastor about the situation? If not, that's what I'd do. After all, they go to them big fancy schools to learn how to deal with just this kind of problem. The other thing y'all could do is switch to a modern hymnal. If she don't know the songs, she can't sing 'em. Or maybe after she's taken her seat, one of y'all could distract her while another person swipes her hymnal. I still think talkin' to the pastor would be the best idea. Let him go and tell her that he spoke with God and he said for her to please hold it down so he can hear the rest of the folks in the pews singin' his praises.

Love, Kisses, and Trailer Park Wishes,
Ruby Ann Boxcar

Volunteer Work

Dear Ruby Ann,

I know the Lord will forgive me for saying this, but the volunteers at our church are incompetent. And it shows. I love our church and our pastor, but I've about had it. I've volunteered myself, but the people who were in charge of the duties that I was doing had no idea what they were doing either. What should I do?

A Frustrated Worshipper

Dear Frustrated Worshipper,

Oh, don't I know what you're talkin' about. We got some idiots at Holier Than Most Baptist Church as well. And the one that comes to mind first is a woman. But don't get me wrong, I'm not one of those folks who gets upset with women holdin' high responsibilities in the church. After all, it was women that Jesus appeared to after his resurrection, and it was women that were the first to go out and spread the Good News. But I really believe deep down in my heart, she was the wrong person to put in charge of last month's Communion service. Poor Deana ain't dumb, but she just don't stop and think before makin' major decisions. She don't have to in her daily life, 'cause she works at a dollar store. I mean, what kind of major decisions does she have to make? If somebody brings up an unmarked item, it ain't like this mentally challenges her. She just rings up a dollar. That's as hard as her workday gets, and trust me when I say that it showed when Communion rolled around that night at church.

Traditionally, since we, just like other Baptist churches, don't do Communion very often, it just don't make sense to have Communion supplies on hand. So the person in charge of Communion goes out and buys whatever might be needed, and then the church reimburses 'em. Now for those of you who ain't taken Communion at a Baptist church, let me tell you what it consists of. Typically you'll have a Communion set which is made up of two to four trays of tiny Communion cups that are a little smaller than a shot glass. There's also two or more small metal plates that hold your crackers. The crackers are usually about the size of a Chiclet. And when it comes to the Communion drink, we use the same thing that Jesus drank back in the Holy Land, Welch's grape juice. Normally you'll have two persons on each side of the church who'll pass out the crackers followed by the small glasses of Welch's. It's pretty simple, pretty cut and dried, and pretty traditional—that is until Deana got her hands on it.

The first mistake that Deana pulled was to ask Phil Naper to usher the Lord's Supper. Phil is as nice as can be, but God love him, at ninety-four his health just ain't as good as it used to be, but we'll get to that in a minute. The second mistake Deana made was when she bought the supplies. Now, our church ain't broke or nothin', which means that her decision to buy a no-name brand grape drink over the blessed Welch's can only be blamed on the simple fact that she's cheap. Oh, but wait, it gets even better. You should've seen Pastor Ida May Bee's face when she took off the Communion lid to pray

over the crackers only to find that the traditional saltines had been re-
placed with buy-one-get-one-free pizza-flavored Goldfish crackers. Of
course Pastor Ida May Bee couldn't just stop the service, after all
there were no other bread items in the kitchen that could replace the
tiny fish-shaped crackers. No, this time around the body of Our Lord
would just have to be represented by those zesty little pepperoni-
flavored treats.

As Nellie Tinkle broke into an inspirational version of "In the
Garden," Pastor Ida May Bee, who was beet red by this time, reluc-
tantly handed the tray of fishes to Old Man Naper. Now everybody
and their dog knows that Old Man Naper has not served Communion
for the past thirteen years on account of him havin' the tremors. The
last time he served, he had to hold the trays with both hands in order
not to spill. Well, his condition had obviously worsened. The minute
he took the tray, it looked like he was holdin' a plate full of Mexican
jumpin' beans. You'd have thought he'd have pulled those little fishes
straight out of the water by the way they was floppin' around. Luckily
Daddy was settin' up front, so he was able to save the day by quickly
takin' the plate from Phil's grasp and passin' it down the row. When
it got to the end of the pew by where Phil was standin', the last person in the bench just turned around and handed it off to the folks behind 'em. All was well, or so we thought. But when Phil went back up
for the tray of low-grade-grape-drink-filled Communion cups, the first
three rows got up and ran. I tell y'all, I ain't seen fear like this since I
was at one of them Gallagher shows. But poor Phil looked like he
was holdin' one of them Wet and Wigglies that you hook up to a garden hose in his hand. By the time someone had gotten the tray away
from him, there was grape drink all over poor Old Man Naper. I'm
tellin' you, there wasn't enough juice left in them glasses to give a
squirrel a drink. And of course, thanks to Deana, there was no extra
grape anything in the back. So after all of us who'd been lucky
enough to set on Old Man Naper's side of the church had eaten our
goldfish, we were forced to go up to Phil and try to suck some of the
grape juice out of his jacket. It was the first time I've ever put Communion, the taste of grape drink, and Ben-Gay ointment together.
Needless to say, Pastor Ida May Bee has assured me that Deana will
never see the sight of the Communion trays up close and personal
again. She put Connie Kay in charge of our next Communion, and I
know as well as I know my name that Connie is gonna manage some
way to tie her Amway products into the whole thing. Lord help us.

But of course, you only got three choices, Frustrated. You can either complain to your pastor, grin and bear it, or come join us at the Holier Than Most Baptist Church.

> Love, Kisses, and Trailer Park Wishes,
> Ruby Ann Boxcar

Dear Ruby Ann,

Recently I have been attendin' a new church in town that I just love. The people are so friendly and kind. The minister is new and since this is his first church to pastor he is eager to do a good job. He has so many great ideas for expanding our ministry and bringing in new members to the congregation. He is always asking for volunteers to go to nursing homes, shelters, hospitals, and all kinds of places to minister and have visitation. But I'm so afraid he is going to up and ask me outright one of these days why I haven't volunteered. I need your advice, Ruby. I think these are real worthy causes and all but some of us don't have time for all of that volunteer stuff. I mean, I go to church every Sunday. Isn't that enough? Between having to be at the unemployment office, see my parole officer, attend my AA meetings, and be at my nighttime incarceration by 7:00 P.M., I barely have enough time to get to bowlin' and my pool tournaments. This leaves me almost no time to socialize with my buddies at the bar, or to see my kids every other weekend. What should I tell him if he asks me to volunteer?

> Busy Beaver

Dear Beaver,

I think I'd beat him to the punch by volunteerin' to do somethin' on Sunday mornin's like usher or greet people or the likes. After all, you're already there on Sundays. And if he asks you to do other stuff durin' the week, just tell him that you ain't got the time. Of course you could also tell him that your private prison ministry, which you don't care to discuss, keeps you pretty busy as well.

> Love, Kisses, and Trailer Park Wishes,
> Ruby Ann Boxcar

Saints and Sinners

Dear Ruby Ann,

I've got this Methodist neighbor that moved in next door about a year ago. She always has a smile on her face and a warm heartfelt Hello, every time I see her, but when she greets you, she likes to give you a hug. Now I've got no problem with hugs. I think hugs are great just as long as your hands are in plain sight. But this gal likes to kind of rock from side to side a bit when she hugs. I don't mind that either, even though that is part of my dilemma. You see, being a good Baptist like yourself, I'm afraid that someone is going see us hugging and rocking from side to side and think that we're dancing. God forbid! I don't want to hurt this dear old woman's feelings, but I also don't want to make someone lose his faith because he thought he saw me dancing.

> Please help.
> A Worried Saint

Dear Worried Saint,

First off, I wish I had that gal as a neighbor! I love a good hug. Second, don't worry about the dancin' thing. It don't count when it's two women like you and your neighbor or two men like Kenny and Donny over in Lot #15. Pastor Ida May Bee says that Baptists don't like the dancin' between a man and a woman or a woman and a man 'cause of what it can lead to, if you know what I mean. Even married folks like me and my husband have to be careful as well. Why, we don't even make love standin' up in fear that somebody might peek through our curtains and think we're dancin'. But it's OK for your neighbor to move you from side to side like she does. So basically just enjoy the good Christian spirit this gal gives you, but remember that as a Baptist, which basically means we're closer to God, you should give that spirit back at least ten times more.

> Love, Kisses, and Trailer Park Wishes,
> Ruby Ann Boxcar

Other Non-Christian Forms of Worship

Dear Ruby Ann Boxcar,

Recently I attended a wedding for a dear friend's daughter. In the middle of the wedding my trusty ol' Lycra girdle gave out on me. Luckily I was towards the back of the church and so were the bathrooms. But I couldn't leave; you see, I was in charge of the guest book. Well, God must have been looking out for me because the church kitchen was right across the hall from the bathroom and there on the counter was a roll of plastic wrap. It took the whole roll but I was able to get back in that dress and go back to the ceremony. The rest of the day went off without a hitch, and I sweated off four pounds and can now fit in the dress without a girdle. However, I feel bad about stealing from a church. What should I do? Replace the roll with a new one, give them the $1.68 it cost, or just forget about it because it is a non-Baptist church (it was Catholic)?

Wrapped up in Wewoka,
Waletta Gae Wood

Dear Waletta Gae,

Hon, I say don't worry about it. After all, that's why they got bingo, ain't it? But I also asked Pastor Ida May Bee what she thought you should do. Bein' the upstandin' spiritual person that she is, she said that clearly that plastic wrap was a miracle in your time of need from the good Lord above, which I agree with wholeheartedly, just like that time God made the sun stand still in the sky. Mind you, Pastor, Ida May Bee says that's the reason behind that daylight savin's thing.

Love, Kisses, and Trailer Park Wishes,
Ruby Ann Boxcar

Church Plays

Dear Ruby Ann,

As a new minister with a new church, I would like to incorporate more drama into our services. I know that people really enjoy the

Christmas play that we put on, so I was thinking about addin' a new play each other month. So, on one Sunday every other month I would set back and the sermon would be done by a group of actors who act out a scene from the Bible. What are your feelings on this topic? Do you think it would work out?

Rev. Peter Cole

Dear Rev. Cole,

We tried adding a new play to our worship service just a few years back when Pastor Hickey was still pastor. It was for Palm Sunday, and it was basically Jesus' entrance into Jerusalem. Since Pastor Hickey wouldn't allow us to have an actual donkey walk into the church, and we couldn't find a man who'd put on a dress and wear a wig and a beard, we had to make do. The Sunday school class had put together some donkey ears and a tail from construction paper, which we put on Me-Ma. We also strapped on to Me-Ma's back a Tickle Me Elmo doll that us women of the Baptist Association of Baptized Ladies (BABL) had dressed up to look like our Lord and Savior. When Pastor Hickey read the Bible passage about how Jesus entered into Jerusalem ridin' on a donkey, Me-Ma came crawlin' on her hands and knees into the sanctuary hee-hawin' down the aisle. Well, with the rest of the congregation wavin' palms in the air and yellin' "Hosanna," it was very movin'. As a matter of fact, most of us in that small rural church were on the verge of tears when our good fortune headed south. You see, no one had thought to take the bat- teries out of that dressed-up Tickle Me Elmo doll before securely safety pinnin' it to the back of Me-Ma's dress. And as luck would have it, the loud sound of our voices along with the vibration of my Me-Ma set Elmo off, causin' it to tickle, and Me-Ma nearly busted a gut. God bless her, she had no idea what was goin' on except that somethin' was on her back and it was movin'. Well, she started buckin' like a horse in a rodeo. And those of us who tried to help her were actually riskin' our own lives. She only had on them little one-fourth-inch bis- cuit heels like she normally wears, but trust me when I tell y'all, if one of them had landed on somebody, they'd have knocked 'em into to- morrow. But that didn't stop some of the menfolk in the congrega- tion that Palm Sunday. They could tell she was panickin' like a deer who'd fallen into a semifrozen pond. They knew that if they didn't help her quickly, she could end up hurtin' herself, as well as others in the church. They also knew the pain that comes from a good deed gone bad as they fell to their knees one by one, after bein' hit by one of Me-Ma's kicks of desperation. Who knows how many would have fallen that day if it hadn't been for the quick thinkin' of Al Hanson, church member and local animal control agent. When the first Good Samaritan went down, Al went runnin' out of the church to quickly reappear with his tranquilizin' gun. Just as Me-Ma had started takin' off her dress, Al let off a shot. The dart had made its home in the buttocks of the crazed old screamin' lady. But she was tough and Elmo was still ridin' her like lint on a pair of corduroy slacks. The second dart, however, brought her to her knees, but before you could say, "Up from the dead he arose," she was back on her feet. The third tranquilizer, as luck would have it, would do the trick, knockin' her out like a light. Within minutes two of the interns from the Last Stop Nursing Home had come by and carted her back to her quiet room so she could safely sleep off the medication. The good news was that Me-Ma didn't remember a thing when she woke up. And of course the other good news was that the whole incident didn't have any effect on the service at all. Once Me-Ma had been put down, so to speak, Pastor Hickey was able to get that Elmo doll off her back, and perform a twenty-minute exorcism on it. Thank God those batteries weren't Eveready or we'd have been there all day long.

So I guess my advice is to do what you want at your church, but just make sure you got a vet on hand at all times.

Love, Kisses, and Trailer Park Wishes,
Ruby Ann Boxcar

Vacation Bible School

Dear Ms. Boxcar,

It is such a pleasure writing you, because I know you will be able to help me. I have been put in charge of crafts for this summer's vacation Bible school at my church. Since you are a good Baptist, as well as active in your church, I thought that maybe you would know some crafts that I could use. The only thing is that the crafts must pertain to some kind of religious theme. Do you have any suggestions?

Rose Fillmore

Dear Rose,

The pleasure is all mine. Yes, I just loved vacation Bible school when I was a child, which is why I still try to help out when I can at the church I attend, Holier Than Most Baptist Church. Last year, under the watchful eye of Pastor Ida May Bee, we had some new crafts for the kids. They beaded dresses and sewed hair onto wig caps. You should have seen the fine craftsmanship of those little tykes. And of course, there was a religious theme with each activity. The beads represented lost souls out in the world, and the needle and string were the child's witness to these sinners. They were able to add each soul to heaven/the dress. It was very touchin'. Those kids were goin' at ramp speed so that no sinner would be lost. As for the wig makin', it was a way of physically illustratin' the verse in Luke 12:7 that says, "But even the very hairs of your head are all numbered. Fear not therefore: ye are of more value than many sparrows." Not only did the kids learn several great life-alterin' lessons that will stay with 'em even as adults, but thanks to the sale of those beaded gowns and hand-made wigs, the Baptist ladies group was able to take an all-expense-paid trip to Worlds of Fun in Kansas City. Next year we're workin' in quilt makin', and as long as no machinery is used, and the children ain't got no makeup on, we think we can legally sell 'em as Amish quilts.

Love, Kisses, and Trailer Park Wishes,
Ruby Ann Boxcar

More Religious Questions

Dear Ruby Ann,

I'm Episcopalian, and my husband is Methodist. What does this make our children?

S.C.

Dear S.C.,

That would make your kids white-gloved bell ringers who can mix up a real good cocktail.

Love, Kisses, and Trailer Park Wishes,
Ruby Ann Boxcar

Dear Ruby Ann,

My dearest grandmother and I have been close since as far back as I can remember. Every year from the time I was eight I would go over to her house and redecorate it for each season. When she had a function to attend she would always ask me to pick out the perfect outfit for her to wear. Grandmother would also get my advice on new hairstyles and take me along when she shopped for art. As you may well guess, I was always happy to help in any way possible. As I said at the beginning, we've always been close, which is why now I find myself a bit troubled.

Every year when one of her grandchildren graduates from high school, she gives that child a new Bible. So when Grandmother handed me this large neatly wrapped box at my graduation party, I knew that I'd find a Bible inside; but what shocked me is that the Bible was white. Grandmother always gives the boys black Bibles and the girls white Bibles. I don't know if she simply ran out of black Bibles or if she did it on purpose. Do you think Grandmother is trying to tell me something?

Sincerely yours,
Christopher Ryan

Dear Christopher,

Let me just say that if life was a game show, your grandma would've just walked off with everything in the showcase, two cars, a boat, a case of Turtle Wax, and a lifetime supply of Rice-A-Roni.

By the way, have you decided what line of work you want to get in to now that you've graduated? With the talents that it sounds like you have, I'd suggest you look into beauty school. You sound like you'd make one humdinger of a cosmetologist, and I know the ever-changin' world of hair and beauty could use you, especially since I've packed my license away.

Love, Kisses, and Trailer Park Wishes,
Ruby Ann Boxcar

Chapter 8

Makeup, Hair, Style, and Fashion

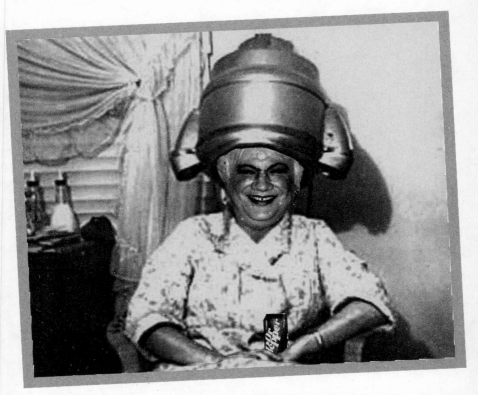

Opal Lamb of Lot #1 enjoys a cold Dr Pepper and pretends she's takin' a trip to the planet Venus while her hair is professionally dried with this hard-to-find Rocket Master Salon 6000 hair dryer, which she got for a song a few years back at a yard sale. Of course, after the last time her hair caught on fire she finally learned not to trust the timer, but to simply shut it off when it smells like somebody is cookin' pork.

*W*e've all heard the old sayin' that beauty is in the eye of the beholder. Well, I got a feelin' that in some cases those beholders are blind as bats. I guess I'm just blessed to have been born with good fashion taste, style, and makeup abilities, and that this blessin' maybe makes me a little bit more perceptive to the everyday world of fashion or lack thereof in some cases. All I know is that my fashion eye is as sensitive as the nose on one of them perfume makers. As a matter of fact, I've had people call me the "Jean Naté of fashion." So it is with that kind of gifted wisdom that I take on some of y'all's questions. And as y'all read on, you'll see some of the troubles that are facin' the world today when it comes to beauty and style. Yes, dear readers, more and more in these days of hardships it seems like the pillar that was once the standard in beauty has become a towerin' inferno (I just love that movie, by the way) as people have thrown caution to the wind, and in most cases it's thrown it back. But as fate would have it, yet again, I am here to save it. I've been given the hose of exquisiteness that can put out that flamin' pillar with one blast of fashion sense. So get ready to cast off those shackles of ugliness, although some of y'all like Opal Lamb will just have to get used to livin' with 'em, because I, Ruby Ann Boxcar, am here today with the key.

And now for your letters.

157

Makeup Tips

Dear Ruby Ann,

I am writing you because you recently gave advice to a friend of mine and you turned her whole life around, so I was hoping you could do the same thing for me. I am not an attractive woman. I can't wear makeup because of my sensitive skin. I was wondering what beauty treatments you are doing that I can try because you always look so nice and fresh. I would love a clean no-makeup look like yours. I look forward to hearing from you.

Signed,
In Need

Dear In Need,

Sister, I truly feel for you, 'cause makeup is so important when it comes to bein' beautiful. And I also am afraid I'm gonna have to burst your bubble. Believe it or not, this "clean no-makeup look" that you mentioned is actually achieved by usin' lots of makeup. I know that it's hard to believe, but it is.

Personally you might want to try some of that hypoallergenic makeup that is all over the market out there. To be honest with you, I had no idea they even made stuff like that until last year when Vance Pool took over the local funeral home and started advertising that only "hypoallergenic cosmetics will be used on your loved one passed, because we care." So go out and give that stuff a try. Actually if you can find it at one of them big department stores you might have 'em give you a makeover and then wait until the next day to buy anything so you can see how it works with your skin. If you're still havin' problems, I'd suggest that you go out and get yourself a can of spray-on wood sealer. Give your face a good coatin' of this stuff and then try applyin' the makeup. That ought to form a nice clear barrier between your skin and the cosmetics.

Love, Kisses, and Trailer Park Wishes,
Ruby Ann Boxcar

Your Coif

Dear Ruby Ann,

I use mayonnaise as a conditioner for my hair. I put the letter "H" for "hair" on the lid and keep it in the fridge. A friend was over for lunch one day and used this jar of mayonnaise on his sandwich. Should I tell him the truth about the mayonnaise?

Darlene

Dear Darlene,

Don't tell him a thing. After all, that's what he gets for usin' mayonnaise instead of Miracle Whip like all the rest of us. Anybody with taste will tell you that the only thing mayonnaise should be used for is hair conditionin' and mayonnaise cake (see my first book, *Ruby Ann's Down Home Trailer Park Cookbook,* for the recipe).

Love, Kisses, and Trailer Park Wishes,
Ruby Ann Boxcar

Dear Ruby Ann,

I, too, am a big gal, and I want to look thinner. I know I can do this with my hair. How high is your hair, and how tall is too tall for a woman?

Signed,
ANS

Dear ANS,

Let me tell you that even the fifty-two-foot giant woman still had a man that loved her, so you can not go too high with your hair. As for me, well, I'm five feet eight inches tall without my hair, and six feet ten inches with it. Somethin' like that.

Love, Kisses, and Trailer Park Wishes,
Ruby Ann Boxcar

Style

Dear Ruby Ann,

My daughter ain't got no kind of style at all. I don't know where she gets her taste, but it sure ain't from me. I tried to learn her good, but all she wants to do is argue with me. So I want your opinion on somethin', 'cause I know she'll listen to you. Is it OK to wear flip-flops with overalls? I know you've been to New York City and all, and are a fashion plate yourself. Please help end this mother-daughter debate. Thanks a heap!

Marleene

Dear Marleene,

OK, you, your daughter, your husband, your pet pig, and anyone else in your family have now been added to my prayer list. Flip-flops with overalls are just fine as long as your toenails don't hang off the rubber sole. If they do, you will need to get out the nail clippers or possibly, in your daughter's case, the wire cutters, and trim the nails back just a bit. Next, add a little style to your day by paintin' your toenails as well. My sister used to have me paint her toenails when I was young, which really ended up helpin' me out years later when I attended the Pangburn Academy of Beauty and Horse Shoeing. I hope this helped.

Love, Kisses, and Trailer Park Wishes,
Ruby Ann Boxcar

Dear Ruby Ann,

I know your readers will identify with my problem. I am not the kind of person who goes around judging people or intentionally hurting people's feelings. But my sister has the most horrible taste of anyone I have ever seen when it comes to clothing. She has always worn the most tasteless outfits and for several years made her own clothes. She's a fifty-something gal with a very large frame. She always wanted to shop at thrift stores even though we always tried to get her to shop at nice stores like Family Dollar and Wal-Mart. I guess she's going through "the change" or something, because now all of a sudden she thinks she's some kind of Britney Spears or Jennifer Lopez. I don't know what's gotten into her! She's wearin' skintight capri pants and midriff tops with no bra! (This is not a good idea when your bust is a 48D.) She lifted her arm to wave at a friend and she looked like an alien life form in a Star Trek Bar. People are starting to talk, and I fear we will be the laughingstock of the whole town. Please tell me what to do!

Sister's Got No Clue

Dear Sister's Got No Clue,

There are only three things you can do:

1. Love her like you would a sister.
2. Get used to it.
3. And thank the good Lord above each day that she ain't a stripper.

Now you know what kind of hell I've had to live through all my life. I've taken your name and your burden and added 'em to my prayer list.

Love, Kisses, and Trailer Park Wishes,
Ruby Ann Boxcar

You're Wearin' That?

Dear Ruby Ann,

It's time for the local Fishing Hole Fry Festival. This year it will be held after 5:00 P.M. What should a girl wear? Can it be a smart black dress or should I risk it with a fabulous aquatic two-piece print dress? Ruby, please help!

Love and admiration,
Tillie from L Town

Dear Tillie,

You know, normally I'd just suggest a comfortable top and pair of capri pants, only 'cause they don't make them dang pants in my size, and I just love the way the word "capri" sounds. But in your case, it sounds like y'all are a little more formal, so I would go with a black tube top that you've either stapled or hot glued plastic flowers to just along the top in the front. Make sure that you don't get them flowers goin' too far on either side or you're likely to rub 'em up under your arm, and that is sure to be painful after a few minutes. I'd go with black stirrup pants simply 'cause you can get those things wet, beat 'em up against a rock, and even run over 'em without hurtin' the dog-gone things a bit. As for shoes, the only answer is bright plastic jelly sandals. Not only will these plastic shoes go great with your plastic flowers, but the water from your fishin' hole can freely flow through the grated sides and tops of the shoes. You will be the filly at the fry if you just go with my fashion ideas, so have fun and know you look better than sugar on grits.

Love, Kisses, and Trailer Park Wishes,
Ruby Ann Boxcar

Dear Ruby Ann,

Please help me decide if my old man is a lying stinkweed or I'm just bein' a suspicious witch. I was helping him clean out his pickup this week, using the long-handled snow brush to snag the Dew cans out from under the seats when I snagged somethin' that weren't no pop can. Hanging off the end of the brush was a pair of silk panties (the kind with the skinny strap up the crack that looks like it would be darn uncomfortable to wear for more than five minutes).

The old man took a look at what I'd found and said, "Thank God you done found my squirrel skivvies!" I said, "What the heck is squir-rel skivvies?" He explains that, when it's plum cold outside, he puts these over his head underneath his hat with the fold-down flaps to keep his head warmer (he said this without so much as cracking a grin). Now, seeing as how we ain't had no squirrel to eat in this house since Reagan was in the White House I'm not real keen on believing this story. What do you think?

Doubtin' Wife

Dear Doubtin' Wife,

I got to tell you that I ain't never heard of anything like that before, but you also got to remember that we ain't white trash, just trailer trash, which means we don't eat varmints like y'all. No, if they don't sell it at the Piggly Wiggly, we don't eat it. So don't take my word on this "squirrel skivvies," although my husband, Dew, is a local guide for tourists who come up to Arkansas to hunt and fish, and he's never heard of 'em before either. But he did say that sometimes durin' winter he has seen men take women's bras and tie 'em around their heads so that the cups are over their ears. This keeps their ears warm, but unlike your everyday ear muff, it ain't thick, so you can still hear while you're in the woods. He also said he's seen some men even put a jockstrap over their nose and mouth to keep their faces warm in the extreme cold. Don't that sound sexy?

Listen, sister, if I was you, I'd make my husband wear them "squirrel skivvies" outside one day when it gets cold. This winter have him put 'em on when he goes to get the mail or has to run to the store. Make him wear 'em in public and you'll see if he was lyin' to you or not. In any case, I'd still leave him. After all, bein' with a man who cheats or a man who wears underwear on his head in public is both humiliatin' and not at all what you agreed to in your weddin' vows.

> Love, Kisses, and Trailer Park Wishes,
> Ruby Ann Boxcar

Ruby Ann,

My front-load Maytag has never been the same since Dicky-Bob, our Doberman, chose to do his business in it and we just can't find the money to replace it. I've had to find other ways to keep the clothes clean and smellin' fresh off the line. Now that I've run outta Brut and Stetson, it's been a trial keepin' my husband's clothes, you know, clean. Can ya give me a few suggestions? Les is tellin' me the boys down at the Stop n' Rob are starting to complain about the stench when his shift is over.

> With much thanks,
> Queenie Calhoun

Dear Queenie,

I think the answer to your question is *laundry soap!* You might try addin' that to the water next time you wash your clothes. But first, I'd fill up the washer with hot water and two cups of bleach. Let it run without clothes in it through a complete wash cycle. Next, do the same thing again, but this time add a regular amount of laundry soap instead of the bleach. Once the wash cycle has ended, go on ahead and start doin' your clothes usin' the laundry soap for each load. If this don't do the trick for you, just give your husband a good blast of Glad, put a car air freshener around his neck, and send him off to work.

Love, Kisses, and Trailer Park Wishes,
Ruby Ann Boxcar

Dear Neighbor,

Is it OK to wear somethin' just because they make it in my size?

Little Linda

Dear Little Linda,

Thank you for your letter. The answer is yes, but only if it covers the important parts of your body, which for you would be everything from the neck down.

Love, Kisses, and Trailer Park Wishes,
Ruby Ann Boxcar

Chapter 9

Travel

The rescue team located Momma Ballzak on the side of Pikes Peak. She was drunk as a skunk, but thank the good Lord she was safe. A couple of bighorn sheep, however, fell off the mountain on account of her breath. They was fine as well.

W hen it comes to travel, you ain't done it till you've had to do it with my mother-in-law, Momma Ballzak. As y'all might recall, she likes to touch the bottle from time to time, actually more like whenever the big hand on the clock is movin'. Well, durin' a recent visit to our holiday trailer in Commerce City, Colorado, my husband decided it would be fun to take out Momma Ballzak and my sister, Donna Sue, who was visitin' and drinkin' at the same time, so they could see some of the sights in Colorado. All I can say is never again.

We took them to Colorado Springs so we could take the train up to Pikes Peak. Now if y'all ever get the chance to give that a shot, take it. Talk about pretty! And of course, it'll be somethin' that you'll never forget. As a matter of fact, I can safely say that the senior citizens' tour group that was on the same train we was on will most likely never forget that trip. Of course what do you expect when Momma Ballzak and Donna Sue each lug on a suitcase full of booze? Those gals drank the entire way up and the entire way down. The brochure says that the entire cog railroad trip, includin' a thirty- to forty-minute rest at the top of the peak takes around three hours and ten minutes, but our adventure was a bit longer. It took our train longer to make it up on account of weight, which I don't understand since it wasn't a full train. Of course the train just flew right down the peak and almost didn't stop at the station on the way back. They blamed that on weight as well, but I can't blame my mother-in-law's liquor bag on that since she'd left all the empties in the trash at the top. I'm thinkin' they need to have that train looked at. It's just like that propeller airplane that all of us rode from

167

Denver to Colorado Springs. Somethin' was wrong with it, too. Why, we had to make three attempts down the runway before it'd lift up off the ground. Anyways, gettin' back to the train ride, since it takes you up to 14,110 feet, some folks tend to get altitude sickness, which can cause vomitin'. Lots of folks on our train came down with a bad case of that. Of course some of the sickness might have been on account of my mother-in-law's halter top poppin' open when she got up to flirt with this one old-timer. She's the only single woman that I know who keeps a full prescription of Viagra in her purse at all times.

When we finally made it to the top, it was beautiful. But then when it came time to go back down, we couldn't find Momma Ballzak anywhere. They had to call in a rescue team to search. It was just horrible. All I could imagine was her lifeless body lyin' at the bottom of the peak. But as luck would have it, they found her one hundred yards down tryin' to feed a bighorn sheep. She had mistook it for a lost cat. Needless to say, I could have killed her. Luckily the rescue team, for the most part, were glad they could help. Did I mention that my sister was able to trade phone numbers with several of the single members of the team? Of course I'm not surprised. After all, you have to remember that these men see horrific disgustin' things every day as they search for lost people in the mountains.

But all in all it was a beautiful experience that I highly recommend just as long as you don't bring your mother-in-law.

And now for your letters.

Vacations

Dear Ruby Ann,

We know that you are a world-famous star and have traveled the globe, so we come to you for advice. My husband, Ned, and I have been saving our whole lives to take this trip and we are so nervous. We have never been anywhere except a few surrounding states, so this is a big deal to us to finally travel abroad. We have our passports, and our shots. We have someone to watch our trailer for us while we're gone and we have stopped the paper and the mail for the next few weeks.

We just have a few questions for traveling abroad that maybe you can help us with before we go.

What do we order to eat if we can't read the menu and the waiter doesn't speak English?

How do we ask where the bathroom is?

How will we know how much we are paying if we are using foreign money?

And most important, what language do they speak in Toronto, Canada?

Signed,
A Couple Abroad

Dear Abroad,

Let me answer your questions in the order that they was asked, OK? Here we go.

1. Spam in any language is still Spam, plus you know it's always a safe and tasty bet.

2. Simply say, "Excuse me, but do you have a toilet in this joint, or do I just need to find a can?"

3. Just hand 'em all the cash you got. They'll give you back what they don't need. Or just put it on your credit or debit card, and let the bank figure it out.

4. Believe it or not, our neighbors in the north speak a lot of American. Just remember that it's rude to correct 'em when they mispronounce some of our words.

Canada is one of my favorite places to visit, and the folks are so friendly you'd swear they all must live in a trailer. Have a nice time, and tell everybody in Toronto that Ruby Ann says, "Hi!"

Love, Kisses, and Trailer Park Wishes,
Ruby Ann Boxcar

Dear Ruby Ann,

I just moved to a new town from Birmingham and am a little homesick. I can't afford to take time away from my new job. How can I make it easier to stick it out till I save up some vacation time? I miss Birmingham something awful.

Flora D.

Dear Flora,

I understand how you feel. As you most likely know, me and my husband, Dew, keep a holiday quad-wide trailer in Commerce City, Colorado, which is just outside of Denver. Since Denver has an international airport and Little Rock's is just a national airport only, it makes it easier for me to catch my flights out of Denver's airport, so when I'm gettin' ready for a tour or such, me and my husband, Dew, occupy the Colorado trailer home. And even though the people in that part of the state are wonderful and treat me real good, I still find that I miss my kinfolks and neighbors back at the High Chaparral Trailer Park in Arkansas. So like I said earlier, I understand how you feel.

All you got to do to make your place feel more like Birmingham while you wait for that vacation time is to simply turn the heat up as high as you can, open up the oven and crank it to broil, and if you got a toaster oven, turn that baby up all the way as well. Then just set around your house, fan yourself, and complain about the heat. In no time at all, and regardless of what the weather is like outside, you'll feel like you was in downtown Birmingham. If that don't put you into hog heaven, then I don't know what will.

> Love, Kisses, and Trailer Park Wishes,
> Ruby Ann Boxcar

Dear Ruby Ann,

The other month when we were going to visit distant cousins, I booked plane seats for me, my wife, and our kid. When we got to the airport to check in they told us we couldn't bring our kid with us, something about not letting goats on the plane. Needless to say if he didn't go (he's been a loyal family member—more loyal than the in-laws), we weren't going either. The airplane company will not refund our (nonrefundable) tickets. Should we sue?

> Signed,
> Grounded Goat at the Gate

Dear Grounded,

Well, I hate to tell you this, but nonrefundable tickets are just that. You could sue, but it'd be a waste of your time and cost you even more money. Of course it does go to show what I've always said. You can't do anything once you've got kids.

> Love, Kisses, and Trailer Park Wishes,
> Ruby Ann Boxcar

Dear Sexy Thing,

I will soon be taking a vacation and need some advice. Actually it is more like a temporary transfer from the prison I'm in now to a jail in a different state to face additional charges. Accordin' to my lawyer, they will drive me to the prison plane, which will take me on my journey. It'll be a three-hour flight. My question is a two-part question. Number one, will they provide an in-flight movie or will I need to bring my own entertainment, and number two, will they have nuts or other kinds of snacks?

> See You in 5 to 9,
> Prisoner 977622345

Dear 977622345,

I just asked the local experts on prison life—my sister, who's housed more men than San Quentin, and Little Linda, who's seen the inside of a jail more times than Robert Downey, Jr.—and they both agree: No on the nuts and no on the movie. So good luck, and I guess you'll just have to find your own nuts. By the way, Donna Sue wants to know if you're picky when it comes to your women. She's got your number, so I'm sure she'll be contactin' you very soon. If she sends you a photo of herself dressed in a fur bikini, that ain't her, it's Raquel Welch. She fools so many incarcerated men with that, and when they get out, they run to her trailer. When this happens, I can't help but think that these poor fellas have already paid their debt to society. How much more do they have to suffer for their mistakes and shortcomin's?

> Love, Kisses, and Trailer Park Wishes,
> Ruby Ann Boxcar

Dear Ruby Ann,

Which one will give a married couple more bang for the buck, a trip to Dollywood, or a season ticket to the National Hockey League on satellite TV?

> Signed,
> Mad at My Stupid Puck-Loving Husband

Dear Puck-Loving,

The answer is easy as my sister. Dollywood! Not only can you have a good time ridin' the rides and seein' the shows, but I hear that the women who work there are all topless as well.

> Love, Kisses, and Trailer Park Wishes,
> Ruby Ann Boxcar

Dear Puck-Loving,

Just cut that top part off and give it to your husband to read. If that don't get you a vacation to Dollywood, nothin' will. Best of luck, and if you see Dolly, tell her Ruby Ann says, "Hi!"

> *Love, Kisses, and Trailer Park Wishes,*
> *Ruby Ann Boxcar*

Chapter 10

Love

"So many men, so little time."

*e*ven though every time me and my husband, Dew, make love at night and he closes the bedroom curtains and curses the moon-light, I believe that he would admit that love is a beautiful thing. As a matter of fact, I'd be willin' to bet that most folks in the trailer park would say the same thing about love as well, which is one of the reasons we're still puzzled as to how dog-ugly Opal Lamb ever got a boyfriend or a husband for that matter. But when Cupid's arrow pierces your heart, the only thing you can do, until you're able to find a stick to bite down on while you pull that dang thing out like John Wayne in one of them westerns, is to follow your emotions. Bein' emotional has never been a problem for us. If you don't believe me, just watch *COPS*, and you'll see just how emotional we can be.

As you dive into this chapter, you'll notice that most of the folks who seek my specially tuned advice in the field of love have really strong feelin's of love, and then later on, of pure hate. There is no in-between with these people. They either love that person to death or they hate that person so much that they wish he was dead. It's kind of like watermelon. You just love to eat that stuff, but you hate cleanin' up the mess afterward.

And now for your letters.

Lookin' for Love

Dear Ruby Ann,

I am a single woman of forty-five, and I just can't meet anyone that I find interesting. I recently was watching *America's Most Wanted* when I got the idea that maybe the way for me to find a man would be to write one in prison. I don't want to be called an old maid anymore and I hear that some prisoners have conjugal visits so it would not be a romance-free relationship and I would always know where he is at night. What advice can you give me, as I am desperate?

Signed,
Desperately Seeking Misdemeanors

Dear DSM,

If you've read my books, you know that when it comes to prison romances, my sister is the warden of love. Why, Donna Sue has dated so many men with records as long as your arm that when bounty hunters pass by our way, they naturally start off their search at my sister's trailer. I can't begin to tell you how many Crime Stopper checks me and other members of the High Chaparral Trailer Park have cashed thanks to Donna Sue's taste in men.

I guess the best advice on datin' someone in prison that I can share with you would be that regardless of how much the fella tells you he loves you, and regardless of how many promises he makes about what y'all will do with your lives when he finally gets out, somebody else in that prison is wearin' the brooch that should rightfully belong to you. The other thing I'd advise is that you contact my sister at *donnasuelot6@aol.com* and see what she says.

Love, Kisses, and Trailer Park Wishes,
Ruby Ann Boxcar

Dear Ruby Ann,

Me and my boyfriend have been together for almost three years. We make good money and have nice cars and a great trailer to live in. I want to get married. The problem is he's never asked me to marry him. How do I get him to propose?

Bobbie

Dear Bobbie,

The first thing to do is to cut him off in the biblical sense. And when he asks what's goin' on, just tell him that you've decided to wait until y'all are married. If that don't work, then just eat a couple of boxes of Ho Hos or Ding Dongs and wait till they put a few noticeable pounds on, and then just fake mornin' sickness till you get that ring. If he insists you go see a doctor, tell him that regardless of what your sister and two brothers might have done in the past, there ain't no way you're gonna run the risk of embarrassin' your family. You'll go to the doctor when you got that little ring around your lovely finger. You big-boned gals can feel free to use that last line as well. If this don't do it for y'all, then just pack your bags, go back to your folks' trailer, and eat another box of them cream-filled cake desserts. At least you know what you're gettin' with them things.

> Love, Kisses, and Trailer Park Wishes,
> Ruby Ann Boxcar

Dear Ruby Ann,

I'm a twenty-eight-year-old man and I'm lookin' for a wife. My mother says I should be lookin' for a good girl at our many church socials; my dad says I should try to find a wife that is more exotic and can cook. What do you think?

> Delmar

Dear Delmar,

First off, I suggest you find yourself a nice Baptist church to attend. That'd not only solve your problem, but it'd make both your parents happy in the long run. After all, everybody knows that all good Baptist women know how to cook and are always happy to show off those talents at church potlucks. And as far as exotic goes, just put an open bottle of booze in the closet and ask your wife to do you a favor and look in there for your good huntin' cap. Trust me, five minutes in the closet with an open bottle of liquor will make any good ol' Baptist a little exotic! If you don't believe me, come on over to the High Chaparral Trailer Park when we start our spring cleanin'. We tend to all be some of the most friendly, exotic folks y'all will ever meet durin' that time of year.

> Love, Kisses, and Trailer Park Wishes,
> Ruby Ann Boxcar

Dear Ruby Ann,

Is it wrong to be in love with Justin Timberlake?

G. Gomez

Dear G.,

Justin who?

Love, Kisses, and Trailer Park Wishes,
Ruby Ann Boxcar

Dear Ruby Ann,

So, I have this boyfriend I've been a seeing for about ten months now. Anyway, we have exchanged keys and all the stuff you do in a relationship. One evening he was really tired and I wasn't, so I just went home instead of staying at his house. The next mornin' I decided I'd go on over and cook breakfast for him to be the nice person I am. To my surprise there was a silver Dodge Durango in my spot in the driveway. I knew it was the vehicle of the nasty ex-girlfriend he went out with right before me. I paced the yard for a good minute to gain my composure. This tramp is as big as a 50¢ piece and even though I knew I could take her, I ain't going to jail for no one. Tom just so happens to have a foghorn doorbell that can wake the whole neighborhood. It was 7:30 A.M., and here's what I did. I quietly unlocked his front door, rang the doorbell, and then rushed into his bedroom. They looked like two cats hanging from the ceiling. Now this hillbilly S.O.B. wants me back. Smart man! He keeps blowing up my phone. I'm getting overload warnings from my Internet provider for my e-mail account. Notes and cookies on my doorstep. Should I be scared? I have bought a guard dog and a gun. My question is should I take him back?

Signed,
Former Watermelon Queen

P.S. I didn't go to jail and there was no breakfast served. The 50¢ piece is still alive.

Dear Former Watermelon Queen,

You should talk to him and tell him that if he wants you back, he is gonna have to prove that he means business. The first thing he is gonna have to do is go over to his girlfriend's house and slash all the tires on her Dodge Durango with that hunting knife of his. Then ask him if he can do it. When he says yes, tell him that you want him to do it tonight, and let him know that you will park your car down the road just so you can watch. You don't want him to talk to her at all. He just needs to pull up in front of her house, take out the knife, slash her tires, and then leave. It's that simple. After he gives you his word, tell him that he will get that kiss that he wants after his ex's tires are flat. When he leaves, call up the girlfriend and tell her about all the calls and such. Let her know that you don't want him and that you aren't mad at her for what she done. Then tell her that the only reason you called is because he told you he was goin' over to her house that night and with his huntin' knife. Tell her to call the police. After you tell her to be careful, hang up. Not only will this take care of the calls and e-mails, but when your old boyfriend gets out of jail for attempted assault/murder maybe he will be a changed man ready for marriage. Little Linda and Donna Sue both agree that jailbirds are better boyfriends.

> Love, Kisses, and Trailer Park Wishes,
> Ruby Ann Boxcar

Dear Ruby Ann,

How do you know if your daughter's latest boyfriend is an unrecognized genius or just another in a long string of pathetic losers?

> Signed,
> Skeptical Mother

Dear Skeptical,

You'll just have to wait and see. I asked around the trailer park, and none of us can be of any help to you since there ain't none of us who've ever known a genius, recognized or not.

> Love, Kisses, and Trailer Park Wishes,
> Ruby Ann Boxcar

Torn Between Two Lovers

Dear Ruby Ann,

Torn between two lovers and feelin' the fool here! Bubba makes my heart quiver like a tuning fork whenever I see him, but Momma and them don't want me to have nothing to do with him—he really ain't so bad, got most of his own teeth, only been in jail twice, made it all the way through tenth grade. He always makes sure to call me whenever he goes out with another girl so I don't worry.

Momma wants me to be steady on Ralphie Joe, but just 'cause he's in line to be the assistant night manager at the Dairy Queen, and all she can see are the dollar signs on his paycheck. Ralphie doesn't make me swoon the way Bubba does, but I do know he could put me in a double wide (national name brand) very soon and I find myself already picking out curtains at the Wal-Mart. Then I see Bubba and I forget all about my curtains and roomy home. Was ever a girl in so delicate a position (socially, I mean, not those delicate positions Bubba likes)?

Polly Cadwallader
Bastrop, Texas

Dear Polly,

I need a little bit more clarification if you don't mind. Do I understand correctly that you got a Dairy Queen in your area that is open into the night? Lord knows, I'd almost be tempted to hitch up my trailer and move for that! I just love me a Buster Bar, so I'd have to say go with Ralphie Joe since all Bubba is gonna give you is nothin' but trouble while Ralphie Joe can promise love, money, and frozen dessert treats.

Love, Kisses, and Trailer Park Wishes,
Ruby Ann Boxcar

Pillow Talk

Dear Ruby Ann,

Sleeping with exactly how many people makes you a slut?

M.C.

Dear M.C.,

That all depends on who you ask. Most of us at the High Chaparral Trailer Park have agreed that if you're married, then only one person, but if you ain't married, then seven people in one year's time will make you a slut. Of course if you ask the gals over at the Blue Whale Strip Club, they will tell you that as long as you don't sleep with more men in one year than you currently weigh, you ain't a slut. Heck, I don't even know that many men.

> Love, Kisses, and Trailer Park Wishes,
> Ruby Ann Boxcar

Dear Ruby Ann,

I am twenty-five and I want to have sex alllllllll the time. What is going to happen to me when I hit my peak in my forties?

> Scarlett

Dear Scarlett,

Who says you're gonna hit forty? With the way you're goin', your ticker might not make it to thirty. My advice is to do what my sister, Donna Sue, does. You and your partner should drink as much booze as you can before makin' love. Then most likely one of you will pass out before you reach the bedroom. Hey, it's kept her alive!

> Love, Kisses, and Trailer Park Wishes,
> Ruby Ann Boxcar

Dear Ruby Ann,

My sweetheart of thirty years likes making love in funny places, like getting off our horses to lay on a rock in the forest. This hurts my back. When will he grow up?

> Sore Back in the Rockies

Dear Sore Back,

Hey, at least he lets you get off the horse.

Love, Kisses, and Trailer Park Wishes,
Ruby Ann Boxcar

Dear Miss Ruby Ann,

It has been several days since Virgil, he's my husband, has touched me. We've been married two years and he has kind of slacked off in the bedroom. How can I help Virgil, he's my husband, be more aware of my urges? I don't require anything out of the ordinary, but I would at least expect the general working over. I love Virgil, that's my husband. Can you give me some kind of remedy to this bad situation? We don't have any kids. Virgil, he's my husband, doesn't think he's able to have them. At this rate, I'm beginning to not wonder why. Please help.

Ima Falker

Dear Ima,

Luckily I've never had that kind of problem with my husband, Dew, but I did ask around the trailer park and the one answer that seemed most consistent was Nyquil. Accordin' to my neighbors, give Virgil, your husband, a shot of Nyquil and your physical relations with your husband will be brand new. Of course he might not remember anything, but that's all right.

Just remember that lovemakin', regardless if your husband is conscious, is a beautiful thing. I know that my sister, Donna Sue, tends to cry a lot when she makes love. But of course, mace will do that to a person.

Love, Kisses, and Trailer Park Wishes,
Ruby Ann Boxcar

Unlovin' Behavior

Dear Ruby Ann,

My boyfriend and I are at odds. I think that it was completely inappropriate of him to listen to my phone messages while I was in the shower. My opinion is that he should have been in the shower with me. What do you think?

> Sincerely,
> Alone in the Tub

Dear Alone in the Tub,

I don't know who I agree with on this one. Obviously your boyfriend was worried about somethin' or he wouldn't have listened to your messages in the first place. It sounds like y'all need to talk about what is on his mind.

As far as the shower thing goes, just be careful. When me and my husband, Dew, were on our honeymoon, we got the bright idea to take a bath together. Well, I slipped gettin' in, and long story short, if it hadn't been for maid service and the jaws of life, we might still be stuck in that hotel bathtub. Thank the good Lord above that the maid had no idea what DO NOT DISTURB meant.

> Love, Kisses, and Trailer Park Wishes,
> Ruby Ann Boxcar

After the Lovin'

Dear Ruby Ann,

I have been with my current girlfriend for a little over a year. Since I got with her I have gotten several promotions at my job and we have moved into a very nice neighborhood. We have acquired a lot of nice things, and that makes both of us happy. However, we just don't seem to be on the same level when it comes to everything else. She has one friend; I have many and I like to do things with them. She is not passionate about anything; I am passionate about everything I do. I give 100 percent to everything. We just do not have the type of relationship I want to have. She says there isn't anyone better out there, so we should just settle for each other. I have been settling this whole time, but now I have met another girl and I really like her. But there is a problem with her, too. She is crazy. Seriously, she hears voices and the whole nine yards. I don't want to break up with my girlfriend because of this other girl, but I want to do it for myself. The thing is, I don't know how to do it. She doesn't make very good money and she doesn't really have anything. I bought almost everything in the house. Do I give it to her? Do I split it with her? Do I give her everything because I feel so bad? I really need some advice from someone wise like yourself.

Anonymous in Altus

Dear Anonymous in Altus,

You better be glad that you're anonymous or I'd be in Altus snatchin' you bald-headed even as we speak. How dare you say that you've settled all this time? If that's the case, then you should break up with your girlfriend and keep the crazy one, 'cause that's all you deserve, you stupid donkey's behind. If you was settlin', then why on earth did you agree to move in with her? You are right about one thing, y'all are on different levels. You happen to be on the ding-dong level!

Here is what I want you to do first. Go to the middle of a doorway and put your hands on one side of the frame and your feet on the other. Now push real hard until your head pops out from your behind. Now that we've got that taken care of, let's look at the situation as two mature adults. You talk about how you both have a nice house together and nice items together, but then it suddenly becomes your friends and her friend. Why does she only have one friend and you have many? Me and my husband, Dew, have just as many friends 'cause we do things with all of 'em. Sure, Dew is closer to some while I'm closer to others, but they are still both our friends. It sounds like you haven't been willin' to share anything outside of the house with her. You need to call all your friends up and have her call her friend, and go out to eat. Have everybody wear a name tag so your girlfriend can get to know them. When you talk, incorporate your gal into the conversation so she feels welcome. Just make sure that by the time everybody leaves, y'all are one big happy group of pals.

And when it comes to passion, she is obviously passionate about you. Perhaps in her mind you are the one thing that she likes to give 100 percent to. And who cares if she is passionate or not? Just as long as she loves you and stands by you, then who could ask for anything more? Take another look at what you're about to throw away and give it your all this time. And for goodness sakes, ain't you seen *Fatal Attraction*? Get rid of that other gal as soon as you can, unless of course you like rabbit stew.

Love, Kisses, and Trailer Park Wishes,
Ruby Ann Boxcar

Dear Neighbor,

I was going out with a man named Silas for a few weeks and I thought we were gonna move in together. He got along with Donna Sue and the rest of the girls down at the Blue Whale Strip Club real well, and I could trust him around them. (Not an easy thing to do with Donna Sue.) Well, he was out on the road and went though Kansas (the land of dirt). He bought one of those lottery tickets, the scratch-off kind, and won quite a bit of money. I could tell something was up the minute he got back home. He had a new hairpiece—it almost looked like it was his hair too, except on backwards. Then he said he wanted some of that Lasix eye surgery. I thought "Great! He can almost see the future now, his glasses are so darn thick." I thought it might be a nice improvement, but at the same time I was afraid that I wouldn't be as attracted to him since he was going to look so different from when we met. To my surprise, I was more attracted to him than ever, he was now just as cute as can be, and he had the money. Well, we've known each other a long time, and your sister bein' my best friend and all I thought maybe you could help me. You see, now that he has had the Lasik, I think they messed up his eyesight and I want to sue. He says he sees real good now, but he also says he isn't attracted to me no more (so, you know they botched the job)! I am sure that they have mixed up some of the nerve endings or something that helps him see things right. Do you know if they can do a reversal Lasix? Any advice I sure would appreciate!

Little Linda

Dear Little Linda,

I can feel your pain. Actually to be more honest, I can see your pain. It sounds like this fella is nothin' more than another pothole in the highway of love. I'd just tell him that either he gives you so much of that money he just won or you will sue him for palimony. Take whatever he gives you, 'cause if you do sue and win, the lawyers will get most of it. So again, take what you can and forget about his sorry behind. He obviously isn't Mr. Right—but his money is.

Love, Kisses, and Trailer Park Wishes,
Ruby Ann Boxcar

Chapter 11

Money and Loans

Let's see eBay beat these prices.

*t*here is only one thing that seems to be about as mixed up as love, and that's money. For some reason nobody but nobody knows how to handle their money, which might explain why most of us ain't got none. Of course out of all of us, I'd have to say that Kitty Chitwood is probably the best at handlin' her finances. But that talent didn't come with birth. Accordin' to Kitty it was taught to her by her "great-granpappy," Grandpappy Abner, when she was just a little thing no higher than a set of trailer steps. Her grandpappy took her out on a pond on her eighth birthday and gave her a very special present.

"You see this, little Kitty?" her grandpappy asked. "This here is a silver dollar. Do you know what you can get for a silver dollar?"

"No, Grandpappy," Kitty replied.

"You can take this dollar into the store and buy lots and lots of candy," the old man answered. "Would you like to have this silver dollar so you can buy lots of candy?"

"Yes, Grandpappy," Kitty answered back with a gleam in her eye.

"Well, it's yours, but first you've got to go and get it." With that the old man dropped the silver dollar right smack dab in the water. At first eight year old Kitty was shocked with her mouth hangin' open in disbelief.

Is this old man crazy, she wondered to herself. Why would he drop that perfectly good coin into the water like that? As she thought of all the candy that just floated to the bottom of the pond, she began to contemplate how she could retrieve it. If she could just tell her daddy back home where the dollar was, then he could row out and get it for her, although he would want a reward, which meant less candy. That would never do. She would have to do it. After all, she'd swum and played in the pond before, but she'd never been out that far. She didn't ever think she would be able to get down all the way to the bottom, and even if she did, she'd most likely never find it.

"What's wrong little Kitty, don't you like candy?" grandpappy asked, breakin' her concentration.

"Yes, Grandpappy, but . . ."

"No buts, darlin'. If you want that candy money, then you've got to go and get it, plain and simple." Grandpappy was right and Kitty knew it. "I tell you what. I'll tie this here rope around your waist, and you jump in. It ain't no more than ten or twelve feet deep. And if you have any problems or you find the silver dollar, you just tug on the rope, and I'll pull you up quick like. What do you say, little Kitty?" She thought for a second. Surely she could do that, after all Grandpappy would never let her drown or nothin' like that.

"I'll do it, Grandpappy," Kitty said with confidence. It wasn't long until Grandpappy had that rope around her and tied as tight as he could. Then, as he held on to his end, Kitty jumped in. She wouldn't have won any awards for her style, but any thoughts of that were wiped away when the tingle of the crisp cold pond water rushed over her body. Up her little head came out from the water gaspin' for air, with her small tiny feet pedalin' to stay afloat.

"Are you all right, little Kitty?"

"Yes, Grandpappy, I'm OK," Kitty answered.

"Now, just go straight down and start lookin'," Grandpappy instructed as the water lapped against the bobbin' rowboat. "And if you find a turtle, leave it alone, 'cause they'll snap your nose right off."

Kitty took a deep breath and then did as her grandpappy had told her. She kicked and kicked until finally her hand felt the cold mushy mud of the pond bottom. At first she simply felt all around that area of the bottom for the dollar. Then when she felt like she was about to burst, she yanked on the rope. Up she went like a rocket ship to the top.

"Huuuuhhhhhh," Kitty gasped, suckin' in as much fresh air as her lungs would hold.

"Did you find it, girl?"

"No, Grandpappy."

"Did you have your eyes open?"

"No, sir," Kitty replied as she caught her breath.

"Well, then open your eyes, little Kitty, and try to see it. If you try and feel for it, you're just gonna stir up the mud and you'll never find it."

"OK, Grandpappy, I'll try." Kitty knew she only had one more chance until she would be just too tired to dive down again. So Kitty took a deep breath and pushin' off from the boat she hurled her tiny body towards the bottom of the pond. But this time when she felt the chillin' mud, she opened her eyes and viewed the murky water that kind of reminded her for just a split second of her mother's green Jell-O. But she didn't have time for that. She had to find that dollar and she had to find it now. Quickly she looked in front of her, but there was no coin there. Then to her left. It wasn't there either. Where could it be? Maybe it was over on her right side. No, no coin! Her movement in the water began to stir up the mud and the water began to grow hazy with a thick brown cloud of dirt. Then as she felt the pressure buildin' up inside her lungs somethin' caught her eye. It was a ray of light. A quick flash that she hadn't seen before, but where did it come from? There it was, right behind her. It was somethin' shiny? Could that be it? She was just about out of air, but she had to see. Quickly she reached for the object, grabbed hold tightly, and yanked on the rope as if it attached to a church bell on a Sunday. Up she went even faster this time to the surface. Kitty gasped for air and then yelled out.

"I think I got it, Grandpappy, I think I got it!" Afraid she'd drop it back into the pond, she tossed it into the boat.

"Let me see, little Kitty," the old man said as he reached down into the boat, disappearin' from her view. "Well, that looks like a silver dollar to me," Grandpappy said as he rose back up with the coin in his hand. "Now let's get you out of that water." With that, Grandpappy reached down and grabbed hold of the back of Kitty's blouse and pulled her up as if she was as heavy as a six-pack. It wasn't until Kitty, safely in the boat, had reached out to claim her prize that she noticed the shiny black objects on her arm. Quickly she retracted her limb and tried to brush the objects off, but they didn't move.

"Grandpappy! What is it," she screamed as loud as she could.

"Now hold still, honey. It's leeches, and you got 'em all over you." Kitty didn't know what a leech was, but she did know that she wanted them off and she wanted them off right then. Grandpappy reached into the bag that he'd brought and pulled out a container of salt. As he assured her that everything would be all right, he began to pour the salt over the little black creatures, which in turn quickly fell off her skin and into the boat, leavin' little red marks on the areas where they'd been. Shortly after he was sure all the leeches were gone, he handed Kitty, who'd begun to calm down, her silver dollar, and then he picked the black creatures up from the bottom of the boat, tossin' 'em back into the still pond.

The old man started up the engine and began back towards the shore. "You see, little Kitty, money is very special and important. But you have to work for it, just like you did with that dollar. If you work for it, then when you get it, it makes you feel like you've accomplished somethin' special, just like you did today. But when you've got money, you've got to be careful, 'cause them leeches will suck you till you're dry and in the poor house."

That was a lesson that Kitty said she would never forget. Of course she would have most likely remembered it just as much if the old fool had just set her down and told her the dang stuff in the first place. But that's how her grandpappy was. Many years later Kitty would teach him the lesson of penny pinchin' when she threw him in the Last Stop Nursing Home.

And now for your letters.

Buyin' a Trailer

Dear Ms. Boxcar,

I've got a chance to finally move out from under my folks' trailer and into my own. I saw a trailer on eBay up for sale, and with the auction closing in less than a day, there has only been one bid. Currently it's at $26.99 and if it stays at under $100, I can buy it. According to the description, it's a brand-new model that the manufacturer is personally selling. It is a double wide and fully loaded. The only con is that it says it has "some tornado damage." Since the only photo that they show is the very front view of the trailer with the bay windows all boarded up, I don't know what all will have to be fixed, but surely it ain't that much. Plus they've got this real pretty blond girl dressed in a real skimpy bikini standing in front of the trailer in the photo as well. Surely if the damage was that bad, she wouldn't have been so attracted to the trailer to stand that close to it. I'm not stupid, I know she doesn't come with the trailer, but I'm sure that when the girls find out that a single thirty-six-year-old dude has a brand-new trailer, I will have to beat them away with a stick. So do you think this is a good buy? Please answer back quickly since I have less than a day to put my bid in. Thanks.

Dan Stubby

Dear Dan,

I always say you need to see a trailer up close and personal before you buy it. After all, if you've read my last book, *Ruby Ann's Down Home Trailer Park Guide to Livin' Real Good,* then you know all the mess Little Linda went through tryin' to get a trailer without actually seein' it in person. I'd wait unless of course you got money to blow and don't mind blowin' it if you get a piece of junk.

Sister Bertha has had some slight tornado damage done to her trailers in the past as well. The last twister picked it up, shook it around, and then after rippin' out the insides, set it right back down about six miles away. I wouldn't have told you to buy that one either.

As far as chicks and trailers, you bet you're gonna have to beat 'em off with a stick. You will have your pick from a number of beauties. Why, just take a look at any of the photos in this book of the gals from the High Chaparral Trailer Park, and you'll see what kind of women you got to look forward to.

In closin', do what you think is best, but remember that just 'cause you get a trailer, don't mean that you will be livin' out from under your folks' roof. You still got to find a lot to park it on, pay for water, gas, and electric, and don't forget the cable. In any case, best wishes. Oh, and just one more thing, I think you're bettin' against Flora Delight or Little Linda on that eBay trailer, so it will go for under $100.

Love, Kisses, and Trailer Park Wishes,
Ruby Ann Boxcar

Dear Ruby Ann,

I have been wanting to upgrade to a "double wide" but have been having troubles with the loan. Any advice?

Cousin Phil

Dear Cousin Phil,

Even with the interest rates as low as they've been over the past years, people like you and me who got real bad credit still can't seem to get banks to loan us no money even for upgradin' our trailers. Because of this, I've told many people to just keep their eyes out for a used trailer. Since the interest rates are low, people who got money or some kind of credit can buy new trailers cheap, so there are a lot more used trailers out there that ain't sellin' like they used to. So them sellers are havin' to mark the used trailers' prices way down just to unload 'em. Nowadays you can wheel and deal with these folks who have to get out from under their old trailer for one reason or another. Then all you have to do is take that trailer and strip off the entire wall without a door on it, park it right next to your trailer once you've stripped off your wall with the front door on it. Push these two together, run a few rolls of duct tape around the trailers, put a little plastic on the roofs so water don't drip in from where the trailers meet, and you got yourself a new double wide. Best of luck, and enjoy the new upgrade.

Love, Kisses, and Trailer Park Wishes,
Ruby Ann Boxcar

Buyin' a Car

Dear Ruby Ann,

All my life I've dreamed of owning a 1956 DeSoto two-door hardtop. Well, finally one has landed in my lap. I can get this car for $8,000, which is a steal. The body, dash, and seats are just like new. But my wife says I'm an idiot if I buy this car. She hasn't dreamed the same dream that I have. And just because the engine is a riding-lawn-mower engine and there isn't a floorboard so to speak, she doesn't want me to buy my fantasy car. What do you think?

DeSoto Dan

Dear Dan,

You're an idiot.

Love, Kisses, and Trailer Park Wishes,
Ruby Ann Boxcar

Buyin' an Appliance

Dear Ruby Ann,

Is avocado green still in fashion when it comes to kitchen appliances? I'm redoing my kitchen and my husband can get a great deal on an avocado green fridge and stove.

Tammy

Dear Tammy,

That's like askin' if updos and cat-eyed glasses are still in fashion. Of course it is. Tell your husband to buy, buy, buy!

Love, Kisses, and Trailer Park Wishes,
Ruby Ann Boxcar

Loanin' Out Your Good Stuff and Money

Dear Ruby Ann,

I live in a trailer park just like you, and also have several relatives and longtime friends who live here as well. I know being the big star that you are you have had this problem too. My relatives and friends always need to borrow money from me. Sometimes they pay me back, sometimes they don't. It's usually only small amounts, but it sure adds up. They're always just about to get their phone turned off or they need groceries and beer. I just don't know how to say no without hurting their feelings. But I just can't afford to keep dishing out the dough. Can you give me some advice?

B. Gates

Dear B. Gates,

Well, you're right. I too used to have the very same problem that you've described in your letter. It seemed like everyone needed money, and I was the Ruby Ann Boxcar Savings and Loan. At first I didn't mind, but it seemed like that was all I was good for anymore. My close friendships had turned into bankin' relationships instead. Why, every time a friend would stop by it was to ask for money. Finally I came to my senses and did what banks do. I told 'em I'd be happy to loan 'em the money but just for one month and I'd need somethin' to hold on to. Needless to say, they stopped askin' and those that did paid me back right away. Just make sure that the somethin' you're holdin' has already been paid for and that it's of value to that person. Your best bets are anythin' with Elvis on it, items from the Franklin Mint, wrestlin' or roller derby merchandise, Fingerhut credit card, jewelry from Fingerhut, Sam's Club and Costco cards, and eight-track tapes. I promise you that all your worries will be over if you just take my advice on this matter, and don't take firearms, checks, or anythin' with the words Rent-a-Center on it from these people.

Love, Kisses, and Trailer Park Wishes,
Ruby Ann Boxcar

Dear Ruby Ann,

I loaned a good friend a lot of money about a year and a half ago. The problem is that he has shown no interest in paying the money back and has recently started avoiding my phone calls. What do I do to get my money back? He has made it clear that this money is more important than our friendship.

Signed,
Hurt

Dear Hurt,

Just do what we trailer park folks do best. Sue him on *Judge Judy*.

Love, Kisses, and Trailer Park Wishes,
Ruby Ann Boxcar

Dear Ruby Ann,

How do you tell the difference between getting in on the ground floor of a great business opportunity and just flushing your life savings directly into the septic tank?

Signed,
Waiting on a Deal of a Lifetime

Dear Waiting,

Hon, if I knew the answer to that, the credit limit on my Fingerhut card would be more than $150, I can tell you that.

Love, Kisses, and Trailer Park Wishes,
Ruby Ann Boxcar

Your Car and Your Relatives

Dear Ruby Ann,

My nephew wants to use my car for a date. He is seventeen and has his license, but I really don't know if I should trust him or not. He is a very good kid with great grades, but still, it is my car. What do you think? Should I or shouldn't I?

Aunt Jeanie

Dear Aunt Jeanie,

I don't care if Moses came down with a stick in one hand and the Ten Commandments tablets in the other, he ain't borrowin' my car. Nobody, but nobody gets to use my car except for me and my husband, *ever*. And that especially means my family members. Them people ain't right half the time, and I don't care if they are my own flesh and blood. They don't make the car payments or pay for the insurance, so I'm sorry, but no. And I don't care how good kids are, when they get behind the wheel of a car, they turn into a demon seed Tony Stewart wannabe. Even my own simple niece, Lulu Bell, couldn't be trusted with a car.

Back when she was seventeen my sister, Donna Sue, gave her the keys to her car, which at the time was an old 1974 red Pontiac GTO, and sent her to the store to pick up her daily liquor order. The car was old, but it was Donna Sue's pride and joy. Well, long story short, when Lulu Bell returned twenty minutes later, the bumper was gone, the passenger-side door was smashed in, and a taillight was danglin' from the back. When asked, all Lulu Bell could say was that she had driven straight to the store and back. God bless her, I'm sure that's all that did happen in her mind. She was possessed by the same demon that gets all young kids when they get behind the wheel. So again, I got to tell you to just say no to anyone, includin' that nephew that wants to borrow your car. And that goes for motorbikes too.

> Love, Kisses, and Trailer Park Wishes,
> Ruby Ann Boxcar

Taxes

Dear Ruby Ann,

I'm self-employed and never know how much money I'm going to make in the upcoming year, yet the IRS makes me guess my future income and pay the taxes ahead of time in quarterly installments. Then if it turns out that I guessed wrong (an annual occurrence), they penalize me. My question is, do you think that's fair?

> Signed,
> Wrong Again

Dear Wrong Again,

No I don't think that is fair, but they don't call me the Suze Orman of the trailer park world for nothin'. As I see it, you've got two choices so that you don't get charged for payin' too little in the first place.

1. Pay more than you actually think you'll make. In the long run this will cover your behind if you make more. After all, it's always better to get some back than to pay more in.
2. Or keep your annual estimates at the same amount, but get a new job that pays less. If that don't do it, then nothin' will.

Good luck.

> Love, Kisses, and Trailer Park Wishes,
> Ruby Ann Boxcar

Chapter 12

Jail

077319
INDECENT BEHAVIOR
WITH A CITY STATUE
PUBLIC DRUNK

Poor Little Linda, God bless her soul, has been to jail so many times that the sheriff's office gives her discounts on portrait packets.

*b*ack in my day, the first three sentences a child learned to understand were "No it ain't your daddy, but go ahead and unlock the front door anyways," "Stuff this in your pocket, and head for the car," and "Son, I'm afraid your momma has gone on a long trip." Now, even though I never heard one of those used by my parents, all my friends around the trailer park had become used to 'em. Of course the latter was a nice way of sayin' that your momma's doin' time or simply that she's in jail. If it had to do with alcohol or somethin' petty, she'd be out the next day or by the end of the week. And as you can guess, there were lots of folks goin' on trips. Why even my own Pa-Pa went on a trip one time.

It was a breezy September afternoon in 1962 when Anita Biggon's now-deceased momma Fonda Biggon, who lived in the same trailer over in Lot #2 that Anita resides in today, came bangin' on my Me-Ma and Pa-Pa's trailer door like she was tryin' to raise the dead. I was right in the middle of blowin' out my birthday candles when that old cow's knockin' scared us so bad that instead of blowin' I inhaled, suckin' the candle flames into my mouth. My top lip and end of my tongue was burnt for a week. Why, I didn't even get to enjoy the taste of my birthday cake. But gettin' back to the story, when we finally opened the front door to see what all the commotion was about, Fonda told Me-Ma to pick up the phone, 'cause she had an important phone call. We was all on a party line back then, so when the operator came on interruptin' Fonda's conversation with her sister over in Russellville, and said how she had the police on the other end of the line and they needed to talk to Me-Ma,

Fonda did what any normal woman in a trailer park in 1962 would do. She went runnin' from Lot #2 all the way over to Lot #16 screamin' at the top of her lungs, "Dina Lee, Dina Lee, pick up your phone, the police need to talk to you!" As you can guess, by the time Me-Ma finally got the message and placed the receiver to her ear, all the other phones in the FDR Trailer Court, that was the name of what is now the High Chaparral Trailer Park, had been picked up as well. That was a common practice back then, listenin' to other folk's phone calls with a hanky or dish towel over the mouthpiece to muffle any sounds, includin' your own gigglin', when the folks on the other ends started talkin' about their personal lives and problems. But of course, this call was even more important to listen to since it involved the police and the upstandin' pillar of the trailer court, my Me-Ma, Dina Lee. Well, long story short, Pa-Pa, who Me-Ma had sent to the store to pick up some ice for the birthday party, had gotten arrested for shopliftin' athlete's foot medicine. As far back as I can remember, Pa-Pa always had the ugliest feet you'd ever seen. As I grew older I realized that he had a severe case of athlete's foot, but refused to go to the doctor about it. Instead he would just have Me-Ma pick up the over-the-counter stuff for him to medicate with. Well, in this instance, he was out and Me-Ma was busy with my birthday. So what he did was to simply leave the correct amount of cash on the shelf and put the medicine in his pocket 'cause he was too embarrassed to pay for it at the register.

The police told my Me-Ma what happened and that he'd be stayin' in jail until the judge could make it back to town, which would be sometime that next week. Well, three days later, when the judge had made it back, he let Pa-Pa off with a warnin' since he had left the money on the shelf. Still, Pa-Pa was mad as a hornet since his arrest as well as the reason behind the arrest had made the local papers. But Pa-Pa never complained about it. He also never went into another store as long as he lived. Many years later, when this story came back up somehow at a family gatherin', he did admit that he'd gotten even with the police department. When they let him use their own personal facility to bathe each day, Pa-Pa said he was so mad about the whole thing that he rubbed his feet all over the toilet seat, faucets on the sink and bathtub, and even on the doorknob. Oh Pa-Pa, I sure do miss you.

And now for your letters.

Legal Questions

Dear Ruby Ann,

The utility guy planted little yellow flags in my backyard. When I asked him why, he said he's going to dig a ditch across my yard to reach the neighbors to install a phone. Ruby Ann, I'm so frightened they'll dig up Ralph, my dead husband. Should I leave town now, ahead of the sheriff, or kill the utility guy and bury him beside Ralph?

Desperate

Dear Desperate,

Now don't panic or do nothin' any stupider than you've already done. Just pretend like nothin' ever happened. Then when the sheriff comes knockin' on your door and takes you out to see Ralph layin' there in the ditch, just get a mean look on your face, shake your finger at your late husband, and say in a mean voice, "Well, there you are you old son of a gun! I thought you'd run off with that tramp down at the Tastee-Freez and left me to raise them hateful kids of yours all by myself!" When the sheriff asks you what happened, simply tell him that ten years back or however long it was, Ralph said he had to go talk to some man at the Tastee-Freez about some money he had borrowed from him. All this time you thought that was just an excuse for him to run off with that blond gal who up and left town around the same time. Now if there wasn't a blond gal who up and left, then put him leavin' with somebody else who up and left your town around the same time. Every town is always havin' somebody up and leave, so that should be no problem. Anyways, just tell 'em you never reported him missin' on account of the shame you held inside for all these years. This would be a good time to cry by the way. So good luck, and best wishes. Whatever occurs, if worse comes to worst, you can still order my books in prison, so you see, all hope is not lost. Take care.

Love, Kisses, and Trailer Park Wishes,
Ruby Ann Boxcar

The Bail Bondsman Is Your Friend

Dear Ruby Ann,

The bail bondsman said he can give me discounted rates if I, shall we say, play house with him. Is that a common practice?

A Good Aunt

Dear Good Aunt,

I checked, yet again, with the expert on jail and all things relevant, Little Linda, and she sent me to my sister, Donna Sue. (I guess since Little Linda's expertise is more along the lines of what happens inside the jail, she couldn't be of any help this time.) When I got a hold of Donna Sue, she said that no, this is not a common practice in the bail bondsman world. As a matter of fact, when she did try this maneuver, it ended up costin' her even more money for the bond than the judge had set.

Love, Kisses, and Trailer Park Wishes,
Ruby Ann Boxcar

Who Gets What When a Relative Does Time

Dear Ruby Ann,

I hope you can solve a family crisis. Grandma is the sweetest person God ever put on this earth. Whenever anyone was sickly Grandma was always there. She took care of her parents and Grandpa's folks until they died. She took care of all of her sisters and brothers till they died as well. She was our family's Florence Nightingale. The poor thing didn't know you couldn't keep collectin' that Social Security on all them deceased people for all these years. She just considered it payment for all her hard work and sacrifice. But the feds caught up with her and off she went to the slammer. Grandma, who is seventy-three, was sentenced to twenty years for fraud. As you can imagine, our families were all shocked, horrified, and embarrassed by this. We were humiliated, and our family name was slandered across the front pages of our paper!

Now we just don't know how to divvy up her estate. The old gal has quite a bankroll after all these years, but we don't know how much should go to each of the families—since we don't rightly know how much each of the deceased was drawin' in Social Security. Then we also don't know how to divide the interest on the CDs and mutual funds, stocks, and bonds. Then of course we have to figure out who is gettin' ownership of the trailer park and shoppin' center Grandma bought last year. Please help us, Ruby, before it gets ugly!

Humiliated and Rich Grandkids

Dear H and R,

Shame on y'all! There your old gray-headed granny sets locked up in a prison cell and all y'all can think about is money! Your granny should be the first thing on your mind; after all she is your kinfolk. You need to make sure that Granny has money in prison for things like junk food and smokes. So you need to figure she'll need about $10 a month for twelve months multiplied by twenty years is $2,400. Set that aside for her. Then you got to figure what is gonna happen to your granny when she gets out of jail. Where is she gonna live? Since none of y'all will most likely want an ex-convict livin' with you, you'll have to set some money aside for that as well. So if your granny is seventy-three now, and she gets out in twenty years, she will be ninety-three, which means if she's lucky she'll have maybe another year to live. That means y'all will need enough money set aside for her to live in a nursin' home for a year, or about $500 if you go the cheap route. Of course you could set her up so she breaks her probation and then the tax payers can continue to take care of her till the Lord takes her home and out of that cell. That's up to y'all.

As far as dividin' her wealth, well, I personally can help you with that burden. All y'all need to do is get everything together on one piece of paper, and send it to me. I will make sure that everybody in the families gets an equal share. Of course I understand that the last thing a family whose granny has just gone up the river wants is more headaches and heartbreaks, which is why I feel it's my Christian duty to offer my help, so I'll take care of all this mess for just 20 percent off the top. After all, why should y'all have to deal with all this right now? So just call me at (***) ***-**** and I'll give you the address y'all can send the information to.

Love, Kisses, and Trailer Park Wishes,
Ruby Ann Boxcar

Gettin' Out

Dear Ms. Boxcar,

During a family fight a few years ago out on Snopes Road Bridge, my son, Eddy-Rex, up and shot his daddy. He's about to get out of prison now and wants to come home. I want to help, as he lost an eye in a prison food fight and don't see so good anymore. But he's been makin' strange comments to me when I visit, tellin' me how with his vision all messed up he sees me in a whole new way. Last week he said he wanted to give me a ring when he gets out to celebrate our new family life. I'm awful concerned. What to do?

Wanda-Jo Casta
Spurlin, Texas

Dear Wanda-Jo,

The answer to your problem is simple. Move! Get the heck out of there just as soon as you can! Don't look back! Don't ever call nobody in that town again! Just hitch up the trailer and get out of there as fast as you can! Good luck.

Love, Kisses, and Trailer Park Wishes,
Ruby Ann Boxcar

Dear Mrs. Boxcar,

I am fourteen years old and my dad recently got out of prison, and I am having a hard time adjusting to him being back in the house with us. My husband had never met my dad until he came back and I barely remember him myself. He was gone for nine years. It just doesn't seem right that he can come back after all that time and act like he is my daddy. I am a grown married woman now and he wants to treat me like a kid. I just need advice as to what Momma should do. Kick him out, stay with him, what?

Shalanda Mack

Dear Shalanda,

Hon, it sounds like the problem is with you. For some reason you feel uncomfortable with your daddy in the house. That is somethin' you're gonna have to deal with. You might start tapin' off *Oprah* and rewatchin' them shows of hers to try and get in touch with your feelin's. But I got to tell you that I think it's high time you and your husband move out. After all, you're a grown woman now, and your momma and daddy need this time to try and rebound or jump-start their relationship. I suggest that you and your mister pack up your stuff and move out into the toolshed or someplace that ain't in your folk's home. I think it was great that you and your husband helped out while your daddy was gone, but he has returned.

Love, Kisses, and Trailer Park Wishes,
Ruby Ann Boxcar

Chapter 13

Work

Bein' a star and a beauty ain't the kind of easy work that most people think it is.

*y*ou know, luckily I really ain't never had one of them jobs where I had to work with people I disliked. I guess that was the advantage I got for goin' straight from high school to beauty school and then after graduation, gettin' to do hair and makeup wherever and with whomever I wanted. Sure, when I was younger I held summer jobs, but I was so well liked that nobody ever treated me in a hateful way. So I asked other folks in the High Chaparral if they've ever had bad jobs or a mean work-related story that I could share about what it's like to work in this part of the world, and unfortunately for this section, they all had the same basic experience as me when it came to the local workforce. Personally, I think it's all 'cause everybody in this area is so nice and kindhearted that everyone loves or at least enjoys their jobs, their employers, coworkers, and employees. It's kind of like Disneyland, except for the fact that the mice are real.

Of course, I didn't let the fact that I didn't have any personal-experience feelin' about work hinder me from givin' out advice. After all, if Dr. Phil can advise overweight women with hair, then I can help y'all with your questions about the workforce.

And now for your letters.

Your Job

Dear Ruby Ann,

What's the best way to go about choosing a career?

S.C.

Dear S.C.,

Look in the classified and see what's available. Don't forget doctor, lawyer, and travel agent all require some schoolin'. Pick whichever other ones sound good and try them. Remember that if you don't like it, you can always just walk off the job, don't show up, or sue the company for somethin' or other. Once you've found one of them vacant jobs that you like, make that your career. This way is so much easier than what other folks will advise.

Love, Kisses, and Trailer Park Wishes,
Ruby Ann Boxcar

Dear Neighbor,

I have heard that vodka is not easy to smell on your breath. Is it wrong to drink vodka while I am workin' at the Beauty Barge durin' the day? All I do is answer the phones and make the appointments. It ain't like I actually touch anybody's hair or do bikini waxes or nothin'.

Little Linda

Dear Little Linda,

Bein' the good Baptist that I am, I'd say no, you shouldn't drink at work, but Pastor Ida May Bee tells me that the Bible says in 1 Timothy 5:23 that you should "Drink no longer water, but use a little wine for thy stomach's sake and thine often infirmities." So in other words, as long as you mix your vodka with wine, you can drink it durin' the day without a problem. Cheers.

Love, Kisses, and Trailer Park Wishes,
Ruby Ann Boxcar

Sexual Harassment

Dear Ruby Ann,

After twelve years of retirement, I'm having to return to the workforce because of the economy. I'm a bit nervous and somewhat confused on a few business-related items. You see, from 1953 up until I retired, I worked by myself as a lighthouse keeper, which I truly enjoyed. But beginning next week I will be starting in a customer service position at a local grocery store. I'm just learning about work-related items and such, like a 401(k) plan or free counseling for employees. And to be honest with you, there are some of these things that I don't understand exactly how they work, but I'm afraid to ask my boss about them because I might end up looking like a fool. So I hope you can answer my questions. I'm just hearing about this on-the-job sexual harassment thing and was wondering if I need to sign up for this like I do for the insurance or will it happen automatically like our paid holidays? And do I have to wait ninety days until I'm eligible for it as well?

> Thanks for your time,
> J.H.

Dear J.H.,

Let me guess, you're a drinker ain't you?

> Love, Kisses, and Trailer Park Wishes,
> Ruby Ann Boxcar

Datin' a Coworker

Dear Ruby Ann,

I have a problem with dating a coworker. I started to see someone from my work about a month ago and now the rumor mill is running rampant. He and I never do anything at work and we are completely professional, but people keep on talking. I really don't think that it is any of their business—seeing as how they can barely handle any of their own problems, why do they have to stick their noses in my personal life? What should I say to make them stop talking about my relationship?

> J.E.M.

Dear J.E.M.,

I know what you're goin' through. My mother-in-law, Momma Ballzak, recently went through the same thing down at the flea market. It
seems that she's always helpin' out the older fella who runs the booth
next to hers, and even started carpoolin' with him as well. You can
imagine how upset she was when the rumors started swirlin' around
the flea market that they was a item. Anyways, long story short, she
nipped the whole thing right in the bud. She did what I suggest you
do. Just tell everybody at your work that you're a lesbian. Needless to
say, now she spends all the time she wants to with that old man without havin' to worry about any tongues waggin'. Of course she does
have to keep her Lucky Strike cigarettes rolled up in her sleeve and
drink Schlitz or Old Milwaukee when she's at the flea market, but accordin' to her, it's well worth it.

Love, Kisses, and Trailer Park Wishes,
Ruby Ann Boxcar

Office Supplies

Dear Ruby Ann,

My husband works for the same company I do. He found out I'm
responsible for petty cash and stamps and sneaks in my office at
noon to steal stamps! (The cash box is locked, praise the Lord.) What
on earth can I do?

Disgusted

Dear Disgusted,

Do what every other red blooded American woman does when
her husband falls asleep in the recliner, go through his pants! Take
out either the money or the stamps if he brung 'em home with him.
If he's just takin' a few stamps at a time, go through his pockets and
count out the amount you need in all the loose change he keeps in
them pants of his. Just remember that the last thing you want to do is
tell him to stay out of your office. You don't need the headache or the
trouble at home. Of course if I was you, I'd lock the office door a lit-

tle bit before noon and pretend you ain't inside. In any case, I'd still go through his wallet at night.

Love, Kisses, and Trailer Park Wishes,
Ruby Ann Boxcar

Fellow Employees

Dear Ruby Ann,

My coworkers and I are striving to improve our performance at work. Effective immediately, we will no longer leave work one hour early for margaritas on the rocks. We will leave one hour early for frozen margaritas, thus cutting our alcohol consumption in half. Is it realistic to see our job performance increase by 50 percent?

Weebee Lushes

Dear Lushes,

You'd think so, but I can tell you that it ain't true over at the Blue Whale Strip Club. One night the owner, Melba Toast, decided that the dancers wouldn't be allowed to drink durin' business hours. As you can guess, that was a mess. You can only imagine how bad the gals danced when they could actually see the trash that was in there watchin' 'em strip. Their performances suffered, as did the morale of everybody workin' there. So from that night on Melba has allowed the bartender to serve the gals durin' business hours. Of course, the gals also started bringin' their own bottles of booze to work. If you find that the lack of drinkin' don't help, then I guess you might do what the Blue Whale Girls do, and do often.

Love, Kisses, and Trailer Park Wishes,
Ruby Ann Boxcar

Work Ethics

Dear Ruby Ann,

Is it OK to call in sick even if you're OK (physically, that is)? Please advise in regard to both work and social obligations.

Thanks for the help,

M.

Dear M.,

Callin' in sick to work or any other commitment when nothin' is wrong with you is just plain wrong, wrong, wrong, unless it's to attend one of my book signin's or public appearances.

Love, Kisses, and Trailer Park Wishes,
Ruby Ann Boxcar

Chapter 14

Houseguests

*When the nursin' home where we keep Me-Ma has to close down to fumi-
gate and spray for lice, she almost always stays with Momma, who can be
seen here watchin' Me-Ma while she soaks her feet. Momma has to keep
an eye on her or the old woman will forget where she is and drink her
soakin' water.*

I always enjoy bein' surrounded by my family and friends, but when it comes to stayin' over at my trailer, well, I draw the line at more than a week. My reason for this is just that when I got someone under my roof, I feel like I have to be the gracious hostess all the dang time, and even though I'm nicer than anyone y'all will ever meet, I do have my moments when I need to just take off my all-in-one girdle, kick off my flats, and run around in nothin' but a caftan. I'm just that kind of way. Why, once after a long week of jet settin' I decided to just lay around the trailer in just what the good Lord gave me, if you know what I mean, but it made the dogs sick, so I just threw on a house robe or caftan. And of course you can't do that when you've got houseguests, now can you? No, I can't just set down in the livin' room and watch *The Price Is Right* when a friend of ours from someplace in the world is reclined in the Laz-Z-Boy across from me. First off, they expect more from me, and second, I don't want to cause them to miss out on heaven 'cause my near nakedness made them lust in their hearts. And even though I know for my husband, Dew, I'm a trophy wife, I'd never want him to think that I was tryin' to tease any of our guests with my beauty. I ain't like that, and I don't condone that kind of behavior neither. Like I say, I don't care how much milk your cow produces, it don't mean everybody needs to taste it. So if you get an open invite to ever come and be a houseguest at me and my husband, Dew's trailer, don't plan on stayin' longer than a week, 'cause you won't.

And now for your letters.

Family

Dear Ruby Ann,

I have a cousin who we call Girtie, she weighs about 485 pounds, and has a serious eye condition that makes her eyes so crossed it looks like she just has one eye. Well, Girtie wants to come and visit me this summer, but I am stumped on where to take her. The last time she was in town, we took her to a Merle Haggard concert (she ain't never been nowhere, and don't know how to act). So when she saw some women throwing underwear up onstage, she thought it was what we do here in Michigan. I glanced over at her and noticed she was swaying to the music and clicking her one good finger, and next thing I knew she was wiggling and grunting and came right out of those XXXXL panties of hers. I hollered out, "Don't do it GIR-TIEEEEEE," but it was too late. She heaved those XXXXL panties at the stage, just like she was tossing a hay bail, just about the same time the big cooling fan kicked on. Now I don't know if you all have ever seen a pair of panties that big or not, but I will never forget the look of terror on them boys' faces—they was clawing and scratching, and batting at the panties with their instruments but couldn't stop them from landing on poor ole Merle. He never knew what hit him. He was screaming and kicking and begging for help. Ole Girtie thought he was getting passionate, and she tried to climb up onstage. To make a long story short, they decided not to press charges on Ole Girt for indecent exposure if she promised to never show up to a concert again. Any suggestions?

Emma Sue

Dear Emma Sue,

You've basically just described why my sister, Donna Sue, ain't allowed to attend the New Year's Eve gospel singin' they got in Conway no more. Boy, that was a mess, I can tell you.

Anyways, why don't you just ask her what she wants to do? Let her decide what's best for her. After all, she knows what she likes and what she can physically do, although I would draw the line at climbin' since you never said if she was actually able to make it up onstage or not. Amusement parks can be real fun as well. She can have a good time lookin' through the shops, samplin' the large selection of foods, and enjoyin' most of the rides. Of course the key words in that sentence are "enjoyin' most of the rides." There will be some rides that she won't be able to ride, and usually she can just ask one of the employees workin' that area if she will have any trouble fittin' in the seats. There are some parks who've put actual seats outside the rides' entrances so you can see if you'll fit in 'em or not without havin' to wait in line for thirty minutes to find that you couldn't get your behind in that dang thing if you'd lubed yourself up with a can of Crisco. For me, these pre-ride coaster seats like Universal Studios, which I recently visited, puts outside the Double Dragon entrance saves big folks a lot of unneeded embarrassment. In my case, it only took seconds for me to see that I wasn't gonna fit in that seat, so I didn't get in line for the ride. Of course it took about forty minutes for the fire department to get what I was able to get in that tester seat out. Can you imagine how embarrassed I'd have been if that'd happened on the actual ride? Me not bein' able to fit in that coaster seat would've closed Double Dragon down for all that time. This way, folks were still able to get in line even though they did have to kind of step over the emergency equipment that the firemen were usin' at the ride's entrance to get me out of that dang tester chair.

Regardless of what you do when she comes in to town, just remember to have fun with her. After all, y'all are kin, so forget what happened in the past at that concert. I know I'm tryin' to wipe that vivid image that your letter created for me right out of my mind.

Love, Kisses, and Trailer Park Wishes,
Ruby Ann Boxcar

Dear Ruby Ann,

What should I do? My older brother is a total pain in my rear. He is twenty-five years old, can't keep a job, and has only been out of prison for a few months. I let him move in with me because I felt sorry for him, and now I can't get him to leave. He has lived with me for six months rent free, and when I asked him to start paying rent he got very upset. He said he felt like he was being taken advantage of. I was completely shocked. I am running out of options. I went so far as to find him another house to live in just to get him the hell out of mine. He wouldn't go. He said that he didn't feel comfortable there.

He always asks me for money, or to borrow my car—and I am tired
of it. I feel as though I have a teenage child living with me. Do you
have any suggestions as to how I can get him out of my house?

Sincerely,
Glutton for Punishment

Dear Glutton,

You've done all you can do. You've been a good Christian as well
as a good sibling. Now all that is left is to give him $25 and ask him
to go to the liquor store to pick up a bottle of his favorite booze. Tell
him that you want to throw the old bottle away, but there is still a
swig or two left in it, and see if he will drink it real quick for you. Of
course after he's done that, give him a big hug and your car to use.
As soon as he has pulled out, call the police and tell them that a
drunk driver nearly ran you off the road and give them the description
of the car your brother is in as well as the direction he is headed. Tell
them they need to stop him before he kills somebody, and if they ask,
give them a fake name. If this don't break his probation and send him
right back to jail for another ten to twenty years, then the illegal substance you put in his pocket when you gave him that good-bye hug
should do the trick. Enjoy your peace and quiet.

Love, Kisses, and Trailer Park Wishes,
Ruby Ann Boxcar

Friends

Dear Ruby Ann,

Recently I invited friends to stay on my houseboat for the weekend. How do you tell your guest that the thong she is wearing is not
flattering on that big ole behind?

Your devoted fan,
Ce Ce LaCroix

Dear Ce Ce,

Your best bet is to invite young children over. They'll do the tellin' for you, especially if you quietly point the "hippo butt" out to 'em.

Love, Kisses, and Trailer Park Wishes,
Ruby Ann Boxcar

Dear Ruby Ann,

How long is a person required to let another person sleep on the sofa?

Signed,
Want My Sofa Back

Dear Want,

It depends on if sex or food are involved. If neither is present, get that lazy, no-good son of a goat out of there.

Love, Kisses, and Trailer Park Wishes,
Ruby Ann Boxcar

Chapter 15

Bad Habits

Nothin' says "Season's Greetings" like openin' a Christmas card envelope that makes your trailer smell like burnt paper and Virginia Slims.

*g*ivin' up smokin' several years back was the last bad habit I finally parted ways with, as long as you don't count the occasional slip of profanity, which is about as rare as a well-acted
Steven Seagal movie, or the once-in-a-blue-moon adult beverage. No,
I've pretty much made my daily habits my diet Coke and food, and the
good Lord knows you can't hurt nobody with them. Of course, stoppin'
smokin' was somewhat hard for me as it is for everyone else that does it,
and even though it was a day of celebration when I'd finally kicked the
habit, it wasn't as glorious, and as far reachin', as when my momma decided it was time to quit.

Let me tell y'all, that old woman smoked like a chimney stack. She
had one and a half cigarettes goin' at all times for as long back as I can
remember. I tell y'all, she smoked so much, my teeth were yellow from
the contact smoke. It was bad. But durin' the past ten years, she started
to slip mentally just a little bit, and it really showed in her smokin' habit.
She would forget to dump the ashtrays, so she'd catch the old filters on
fire. You'd walk in her trailer and it smelled like burnin' butts, just like
Kenny and Donny's trailer over in Lot #15. Or her cigarettes would fall
out of the ashtrays and onto the table. She's still got burn marks all over
her furniture, carpets, her bed, the bathtub, and even on the walls. It
was terrible. She and Daddy are lucky to still be alive, but that didn't
matter to Momma back then. "Oh, well," she'd say out of the corner of
her mouth as she puffed away with that cigarette danglin' from the other
side, "when you got to go, you got to go." I can't begin to tell you how
many Christmas cards, birthday cards, and even letters I got from Momma

with cigarette burns all over 'em. I did everything I could to get her to quit, but oh no, she wouldn't have it.

"When the good Lord sees fit to tell me to stop smokin', Ruby Ann, then I'll stop," she would always answer back. I don't know what kind of a sign she expected to get, but she got one she'd never forgot, I can tell you that. She was in the bathroom, readin' one of her romance novels when she discarded her cigarette butt in the toilet and then picked up a second burnin' smoke out of the ashtray. About twenty seconds later my mother stared to smell smoke and then realized that the cigarette she'd thrown in the toilet had caught the bathroom tissue below her on fire. Accordin' to Daddy, it sounded like somebody had stepped on a cat's tail. She came runnin' out of that bathroom lickety-split. Daddy said she ran over to him in the livin' room and said her behind was on fire. Well, it wasn't, but it had been singed. As you can imagine my prayers had been answered, Momma put the cigarette she was smokin' out and has never lit up another since that night. Of course, from time to time Daddy will still affectionately call her his "little old smoked ham."

Smokers

Dear Ruby Ann,

Are cigars really a sublime pleasure or just another smelly habit?

Signed,
Smoked Out

Dear Smoked,

It really depends on the person in the room. Just remember that one man's vichyssoise is another man's foot water. So basically to each his own.

Love, Kisses, and Trailer Park Wishes,
Ruby Ann Boxcar

Drunks

Dear Ruby Ann,

My uncle is a sloppy drunk. How can I make him put the bottle down?

Nancy Thomas

Dear Nancy,

Did you see my sister's book? If you get the answer, please send it to me.

Love, Kisses, and Trailer Park Wishes,
Ruby Ann Boxcar

Profanity

Dear Ruby Ann,

I know you don't have any children and sometimes you should be thankful for your blessin's. I have four teenagers that are a real handful. Their daddy isn't around much since he works in the oil fields. I make the best of things with him gone so much of the time. I try to raise them in a good Christian home. I teach them right from wrong. I make them get good grades. I make them attend Sunday school and church every week. But lately I just can't keep them from cursing all the damn time. What can I do to make them stop?

Profanity Ain't Proper

Dear Profanity,

Do what my momma did to me, my sister, Donna Sue, and my late brother when we'd swear. Wash them kids' mouths out with soap. If that don't do the trick, move up to Lava, and then Comet if need be.

Love, Kisses, and Trailer Park Wishes,
Ruby Ann Boxcar

Bad English

Dear Ruby Ann,

Is Uncle Dad or Aunt Mom proper English in the backwoods?

Doug Morgan
Mesa AZ

Dear Doug,

Now, I ain't never heard those names used. Are you sure you ain't meanin' the common Uncle Brother, Grandma Sister, or Auntie Uncle?

Love, Kisses, and Trailer Park Wishes,
Ruby Ann Boxcar

Dear Ruby Ann,

I am irritated when people use the words "got" or "gotten" when they mean "receive" or "received." It makes me want to strangle people. What should I do?

Signed,
I Ain't Got Nobody

Dear I Ain't,

I'm sorry, but I don't understand what you've done got yourself all riled up about? I asked around the trailer park and nobody else has got a clue as to what your problem is with "got," "gotten," or either form of "receive." But I am addin' you to my prayer list.

Love, Kisses, and Trailer Park Wishes,
Ruby Ann Boxcar

Others

Dear Ruby Ann,

Love your books. Do you have any tips on getting the sand out of your crack after a day at the beach?

Signed,
Salt Water Phil

Dear Phil,

Shame on you! I can't believe you actually took the time to set down and write me a question like that. How stupid are you? Instead of worryin' about gettin' the sand out of your crack, you need to get the crack out of your life. You don't need all that kind of stuff. Sure, my sister can suck up more liquor than Sponge Bob Square Pants, and forgets who she is from time to time, as do fellow neighbors Faye Faye LaRue, Momma Ballzak, and Little Linda, but when you cross that terrible *Valley of the Dolls* line and start poppin' them pills and messin' with that crack like they was carnival candy, well, it can take you over faster than a tipsy cousin at a family reunion. Since you've read my books, you obviously have taste and a zest for life, so I'm gonna add you to my prayer list in hopes that you'll just say no in the future, and that regardless if you are at the beach or out havin' a good time, you will stay away from that crack.

Love, Kisses, and Trailer Park Wishes,
Ruby Ann Boxcar

Dear Ruby Ann,

I have a question for you about lying. I am a former Miss Peanut Princess and when I was a young girl my mom also entered me in the Miss Dairy Princess pageant. I made it to the top five and it was time for the judges to ask the contestants questions. I should let you know right now I am lactose intolerant and subsequently have never been too fond of dairy products. Well, of course I drew Ms. Valeta Parrish. She had lost the same pageant to my mother many years earlier. But, she had never gotten over it and blamed my mom for all of her own shortcomings. So, knowing I was lactose intolerant and not being a good Christian woman, she asked me if I liked milk. I, being an honest and devout Southern Baptist (like yourself), answered that I did not like milk. To this day my mother tells me I should have just lied and said I love milk. What do you suggest I tell her to get her to let it go. I mean, I think she may be holding on to this as a grudge just because it was Ms. Valeta Parrish that asked me that question to begin with.

Yours truly,
First Runner-up

Dear Runner-up,

Next time somebody asks you a question, think about it before you answer. This old bag asked if you liked milk. She didn't ask if you liked the taste of milk. You can say you love milk because it brings so much pleasure to people all across the world. So basically you blew it, hon. You're lucky your momma didn't beat you into next week for fallin' into that old bag's trick. I know this sounds harsh, but you have to remember I, too, was involved in the pageant system and I know how important the questionin' part of the contest is. As many folks know, when I was in middle school I was named Miss Feeder Hog, Junior Division, at the Arkansas State Fair.

Love, Kisses, and Trailer Park Wishes,
Ruby Ann Boxcar

Dear Ruby Ann,

My grandson has a bad habit, which I fear may ruin his life. Every summer, he comes and stays with me on my big farm in the panhandle of Oklahoma. Lord knows I need the help with the critters and the upkeep, and he's a blessing in that respect because he loves to help his me-ma. Twice a week, I volunteer at the nursing home with my Baptist church group. When I'm gone, my grandson will walk the two miles of our driveway in the late afternoon to check the mail looking for my *TV Guide* and Fingerhut catalogs for me. It's hot as you-know-where in the summer here and he frequently runs around without shoes on until he has to get the mail. Because the driveway is covered in the large rocks from the river, he has to wear shoes to avoid blistering his feet.

Ruby Ann, here's my question. One day I came home from the nursing home early (due to a cafeteria mix-up making most of my church group ill) and I saw my grandson walking back from the mailbox in a pair of his black-sheep aunt's stiletto high heels. I asked him about it and he assured me he's worn a different pair of her devilish shoes each time he checks the mail and that he's done so for as long as he can remember coming to visit me. Ruby Ann, what I worry about is will his wearing high heels navigating two miles of sun-baked blistering river rock–paved driveway harm his developing muscles or injure his ankles permanently? I will get him some orthopedic high heels if necessary to prevent his injury,

A Concerned Me-Ma,
Effie Gee

Dear Effie Gee,

Sister, you've got a problem that you need to deal with immediately. Don't put this one off, 'cause it could affect y'alls future. You need to have that mailbox moved closer to the house. My goodness, hon, who knows what might happen one day while your grandson is out there gettin' the mail. Why, a snake could crawl up and bite him and there he'd be, dyin' all alone 'cause his grandma had to have her mailbox two miles from the house. Or what if a pack of wild dogs or pigs or coyotes came across his path. I don't care if the boy has on a pair of them Naturalizers, he ain't gonna be able to outrun 'em. He's lunch all 'cause his granny has to live like she's doggone Laura Ingalls Wilder. If you'd just have that mailbox moved next to the house, your grandson could go outside and get the mail in seven-and-a-half-inch thigh-high boots without you havin' to worry about his ankles or more important, his safety. And if you want the exercise, join a doggone gym.

Love, Kisses, and Trailer Park Wishes,
Ruby Ann Boxcar

Dear Ruby Ann,

Is it wrong to replace a dead goldfish with a living one and not tell your kids that the first one died? What about a dog?

Cecil Greenhaw

Dear Cecil,

Goldfish, yes, dogs, no, and husbands definitely not.

Love, Kisses, and Trailer Park Wishes,
Ruby Ann Boxcar

Chapter 16

Cookin'

Juanita and Harland Hix take a second to pose for a quick picture just before enjoyin' an anniversary dinner that Juanita slaved all day in the kitchen to make. Needless to say, they went out to the Taco Tackle Shack instead of eatin' the ashes.

$\mathcal{N}$ow, the cookin' part of this book should need no introduction. After all, the only thing y'all have to do is pick up any of my first four books to find out that when it comes to the kitchen part of the trailer home, all us folks at the High Chaparral know what we're talkin' about. Note here, please, that I said "all of us folks at the High Chaparral." My Me-Ma, whose senile idea of a dish from the kitchen is cottage cheese and ketchup sandwiches with a sprinkle of cinnamon, no longer lives at the High Chaparral, but rather at the Last Stop Nursing Home. She ain't been an active part of our community for a long time even though we do get stuck with her on occasions. Yes, the old lady could cook up a storm when she was younger, if you don't count her terrible fudge. But now, well, she's a few ingredients short of a cherry cobbler, if you know what I mean, when it comes to cookin'. Just the other day when I was watchin' her at my trailer, she managed to sneak into the kitchen and cook. Well, I was in my office workin' on this book, and I thought she was asleep in the guest room just down the hall. When I got up and went downstairs to the first floor of my two-story double-wide pink trailer home to get a drink, you can imagine my surprise to see my kitchen lookin' like a twister had hit it.

"What in the heck happened in here," I asked out loud.

"I made us some dessert," my Me-Ma said from under my dinin' room table.

"What kind of dessert," I inquired, almost afraid of what I'd hear back.

Me-Ma crawled out from the table and smiled this big cheesy grin.

She then walked over to the fridge, opened it up, and pulled out a bowl of what could best be described as somethin' you'd empty from your garbage disposal. "Butterscotch spinach puddin' with cherries pieces and curry." I could have lost it right there on my kitchen floor, but I held it in. Heck, I ain't even got curry in my trailer. She just looked so dog-gone proud of what she'd accomplished that all I could do was act like I couldn't wait to eat it. Then I told her to go back up to bed and take a nap after all that hard work she'd done, and I cleaned, OK, I pushed the mess over into the corner. Later that night, when I took her back to the nursin' home, I gave her a kiss goodnight, and thanked her for cookin' that lovely dessert for me and my husband, Dew, to enjoy with our dinner when I got back home. She smiled and assured me that it was her pleasure. As I walked from her room and down those dimly lit hallways towards the entrance doors, I couldn't help but think how special it is to have a grandma that loves you so much, even in her last stages of life, she wants to make somethin' special for you to enjoy. Mind you, I also stopped off at the nurse's desk on the way out and told 'em they needed to double her dosages just as soon as possible.

Kitchen Talk

Dear Ruby Ann,

I married a guy from Texas and agreed to move down here. Man, this is another world. Hubby ridicules me to his family, saying I couldn't cook without a can opener. (Who does? And why is that supposed to be bad?) What do I do about a husband who humiliates me all the time?

Hit in the Face with a Can Opener

Dear Can Opener Face,

This one is simple. You set his big Texas butt in a chair and lay down the law. He has three choices and they are:

1. He finds a better-payin' job so y'all can eat out for every meal.
2. He starts doin' the cookin' himself.
3. He shuts his mouth, eats what you cook, and never makes another comment in public about your cookin'.

Of course, if any of that seems a little drastic for you to do, then we got to turn the attention on you and not your hubby. If you can't do what I suggested above, then you're the one that's gonna have to make some changes instead of him. In order to keep him from talkin' about your cookin' you're gonna need to work on that area. And even though it sounds like you've mastered some dishes, you still could use a little help in the kitchen. As luck would have it, all three of my cookbooks are the answers to a happy marriage for you and your husband. Since all the recipes you find in my books are easy to make, you should have no problem. Why some of 'em even call for cans to be opened, and you know you can do that. If you can boil water and operate a microwave, you should be able to cook most of the temptin', mouth-waterin' dishes you'll find in my books. So if you run into any trouble while usin' my recipes, just drop me an e-mail at *rubylot18@aol.com* or simply go to my Web page at *www.rubyannboxcar.com* and send me an e-mail from there. I'm always happy to help. So good luck, and remember to try somethin' that is easy to make, such as my Sloppy Sloppy Joes, first. Take care, and Happy cookin'!

> Love, Kisses, and Trailer Park Wishes,
> Ruby Ann Boxcar

Dear Ruby Ann,

Every Wednesday afternoon one of us at the Bible study that I attend bring refreshments for the whole group. Normally it's just crackers or chips and a dip. Well, it's my turn and I really want to bring something different, but yet tasty. Do you have a dip recipe that I can try out on my classmates? Thanks.

> Father L.

Dear Father L.,

The answer to your question is, "Yes I do." Back in 2002 when I was invited to appear on *Open Mike Live with Mike Bullard* in Toronto, Canada, my assistant Kevin came across a dip put out by a well-known American company. Needless to say, this stuff was fantastic. When we got back to the States we searched all over the place and couldn't find it. We even contacted the American company that made it, and we were told that unfortunately it ain't a product that they sell in the U.S. Our hearts were broke. What could we do? Well, Kevin ended up makin' several tries at reconstructin' this recipe, and as luck and some good strong Baptist prayers would have it, he finally managed to reproduce it. What kind of dip is it? Good question. The dip is none other than dill pickle dip. Mind you there are lots of dill dips on the market and even a few nasty-tastin' pickle dips on the Web, but we were never able to find a dill pickle dip that tasted as great as this one that we had in Canada until now. So with all that said, here is the recipe, and trust me when I tell you, your Bible study group is gonna go nuts for this stuff.

Kevin's Dill Pickle Dip

This is so good, a Presbyterian would open up a Bible for a second helpin'.

Makes about 1½ cups

> 1 (8-ounce) package cream cheese, softened
> 2 tablespoons sour cream
> 2 tablespoons dill pickle relish (not sweet)
> 2 teaspoons dill weed
> 1 teaspoon onion powder
> 1/4 teaspoon alum

Mix everything together, and refrigerate for at least 2 hours.

Enjoy, Father L.

Love, Kisses, and Trailer Park Wishes,
Ruby Ann Boxcar

Dear Ruby Ann,

I need your advice on how to get fried chicken to be tasty but not too dry. My friends and family won't eat my cooking and they use my biscuits for target practice. The dog won't even touch it.

Signed,
Yan Can't Cook

Dear Yan,

Today is your lucky day, 'cause I got your answer. Grab your local phone book, open it up, find the number for the nearest KFC, and call the colonel for drivin' directions. Normally I'd suggest that you grab one of my cookbooks, but, Yan, if the dog won't touch your food, just give up and eat out!

Love, Kisses, and Trailer Park Wishes,
Ruby Ann Boxcar

Dear Ruby Ann,

What do you think of the Atkins Diet? Should I give it a try?

Gomez

Dear Gomez,

You know, I've tried the Atkins Diet, and lost a lot of weight, but as soon as I got off it, and started eatin' like I normally do, all my weight came back. The Atkins Diet works just as long as you continue to eat that way. But since I ain't your doctor, you should go and talk to them first and see what they say is best for you. I can tell you that durin' that first two weeks of the initiation phase, you'd have thought I was a fire hydrant that some dang kid had opened up. That part I didn't care for. My husband, Dew, our doggies, and close neighbors weren't real happy about it either.

Love, Kisses, and Trailer Park Wishes,
Ruby Ann Boxcar

Dear Ruby Ann,

I am totally enjoying *The Down Home Trailer Park Cookbook.*
And, within the near future plan on purchasing the other three books
so I have the entire set. However, I do have a question. Most of the
recipes call for margarine as the shortening ingredient. I am allergic
to it, therefore, without destroying the recipe, would it be possible to
substitute butter? Or, is there another shortening that is recommended?

Thank you for your help in this matter.

Sincerely,
Ronnie Casey

Dear Ronnie,

Your load and your cross are heavy to bear. Lord bless you, I can't
imagine not bein' able to enjoy the oily taste of margarine. But since
the good Lord has decided that you will never be able to sup from the
Parkay tub, butter will work just fine. Use the same amount of butter
as I use margarine. And know that I've added you to my prayer list in
hopes that they someday find a cure for your allergy.

Love, Kisses, and Trailer Park Wishes,
Ruby Ann Boxcar

Dear Ruby Ann,

Are tomatoes a fruit or a vegetable, and what the hell difference
does it make on a sandwich?

Tommy the Tomato Lover

Dear Tommy,

The answer to the first part of your question is that tomatoes are
a fruit. Actually they're the most popular fruit in the entire world.
They are a fruit because, generally, a fruit is the edible part of the
plant that contains the seeds, while a vegetable is the edible stems,
leaves, and roots of the plant. But with that said, a cherry tomato

don't taste like you're eatin' a cherry and a tomato at the same time, which I found very disappointin'.

The answer to your second part is no, it don't make no kind of difference when it's on a sandwich. If you like the taste, you like the taste.

Love, Kisses, and Trailer Park Wishes,
Ruby Ann Boxcar

Dear Ruby Ann,

Does the expiration date of milk mean that that's the last day the milk is OK to drink or the first day it's no longer OK to drink?

Sally Clark

Dear Sally,

Great question. Most food experts will tell you that milk is still good up to seven days past that expiration date, but me personally, I toss it in the trash when it gets to that date or I pour it in a bowl, cover it up, and when them Jehovah Witnesses, Mormons, or door-to-door salesmen stop by I pass it off with a few crackers as homemade Gorgonzola. God bless 'em, Sally, they don't stay long.

Love, Kisses, and Trailer Park Wishes,
Ruby Ann Boxcar

Dear Ruby Ann,

Good cholesterol, bad cholesterol, high protein, low fat . . . I'm confused about what's healthy to eat anymore. Which of your recipes would you recommend for the health-conscious eater?

Dazed and Confused

Dear Dazed and Confused,

All my recipes are recommended for the health-conscious eater if they lived back in the sixteenth century. But hey, when it's your time to go, it's your time to go, regardless if you're eatin' a sun-dried tomato slice or a rich piece of Lulu Bell's Lemon Tree Cake from my first book.

Love, Kisses, and Trailer Park Wishes,
Ruby Ann Boxcar

Dear Ruby Ann,

My friend told me that Spam really stands for Sphincter–Purée–And–Membranes. Is that really true? I always thought it stood for Spare–Parts–Already–Minced. Please respond quickly—we have tickets to the National Mud Wrestling Championship riding on this.

Hillary and Monica

Dear H and M,

I'm afraid y'all are both wrong, as are all of those folks out there that thought the name stood for "Something Posing As Meat." Spam, which is actually made from pork shoulder, ham, salt, sugar, sodium nitrite, and other spices, gets it name from a contest that Hormel held back in the 1930s to name the new product. Personally the story that I like was that the actor Kenneth Daigneau, who won the contest, named it after spiced ham. In any case, as everybody will tell you, it's the food of the gods, and of most Hawaiians, who eat more Spam per person than people in any other state. Go figure.

Love, Kisses, and Trailer Park Wishes,
Ruby Ann Boxcar

Dear Ruby Ann,

I have a dear friend who wants my secret recipe for monkey bread. I don't share my recipes. Would it be OK to give her the recipe but leave out an ingredient?

Marsha, Cell Block 57

Dear Marsha,

Shame on you! Leavin' out an ingredient in a recipe will get you a ticket straight to hell. Where is your humanity and care for your fellow man? Don't be that mean and hateful. Instead, just give her somebody else's plain monkey bread recipe and when it don't come out tastin' the same as yours, publicly insist she must be doin' somethin' wrong or that she just ain't no good in the kitchen.

Love, Kisses, and Trailer Park Wishes,
Ruby Ann Boxcar

Dear Ruby Ann,

Can a man and a woman ever really share a kitchen?

Curious

Dear Curious,

Of course they can, just as long as he follows every direction and order that she gives him.

Love, Kisses, and Trailer Park Wishes,
Ruby Ann Boxcar

Dear Ruby Ann,

What makes brown sugar brown?

Louisa

Dear Louisa,

The answer to your wonderful question is that brown sugar gets its color from molasses. Now what molasses was doin' around the sugar, I don't know.

Love, Kisses, and Trailer Park Wishes,
Ruby Ann Boxcar

Hey, Ruby Ann,

I *really* need your help. I've become a huge fan of your recipe books, but now I find once I start cooking, I can't get people to go home. They just sit there like lawn furniture, eat my food, smoke their Lucky Strikes and clamor for more RC Cola Chicken. I lost my job, I can't get any sleep, and I'm filled with nonstop rage. Day and night all I hear is "Can I get some more of that RC Chicken?" Do you have any recipes to help send unwanted guests home?

Thanks!
Overbooked and Cooked

Dear Overbooked and Cooked,

I know what you mean and what kind of a dilemma my good cookin' can cause. But the answer is an easy one. Next time, try the Born-Again Baked Beans that are in my *BBQin' Cookbook,* and add the Cabbage Roll Casserole from my *Holiday Cookbook* as a backup. That ought to do the trick.

Love, Kisses, and Trailer Park Wishes,
Ruby Ann Boxcar

Dear Ruby Ann,

I have heard about Crisco being used for other things than just cooking fried chicken. I am first of all shocked and second wondering if you can use Wesson oil, or any off-brand vegetable oil also.

Kitchen Kitten

Dear Kitchen Kitten,

I, too, was shocked when I heard about this other use, but I got to tell you, the pie crust is to die for. I'm sure Wesson oil and the other brands would make it flaky as well, but the folks in the trailer park swear by the Crisco, especially my sister. She goes through Crisco faster than I go through Gold Bond. Of course, you can bet your last dollar that she ain't never invited me over for a piece of pie.

Love, Kisses, and Trailer Park Wishes,
Ruby Ann Boxcar

Chapter 17

Culture

No spittin' or chewin' gum disposal, please.

a lot of folks would never guess this, but when it comes to the finer arts, all of us at the trailer park love 'em. I kid you not, we are cultural fanatics. Now, it didn't use to be that way for everybody at the High Chaparral Trailer Park, but it sure is now. I, of course, bein' the world traveler that I am, have always had a taste for the finer things in life. But as far as the rest of the neighborhood goes, well, they all jumped on board the sophistication train a few years back when Kenny and Donny moved into Lot #15. If y'all ever get the chance to meet these two men, you'll understand what I mean when I say they're pure refinement. These two fellas have done more to put us up the social ladder than *Sesame Street* and *The Electric Company* combined. Thanks to Kenny and Donny, we've all become fans of the classics like *Little Women, Moby-Dick, The Scarlet Letter,* and *The Call of the Wild,* just to name a few. Why, we like 'em so much that someday we might even check the books out from the library and read a few pages just to see how close they are to the movie versions that we've come to love.

And how can we thank them enough for turnin' us on to classical music. We most likely wouldn't have never known of these Old World composers if the boys hadn't got us hooked to them Hooked on Classics albums.

And don't even get me started on what they've taught us about fine art. Why, Lois Bunch had no idea that the statue inside her rain lamp was Venus de Milo until Kenny and Donny came around.

So as you can see, you can't always judge a book by its cover. After all, I find that most folks who first pick up my books after viewin' just my photo from a distance, think it's either a book on modelin' or some kind of self-help guide to lovemakin'.

Literature

Dear Ruby Ann,

What books do you recommend that everybody should keep in their homes?

Signed,
The Book Nut

Dear Book Nut,

Here we go.

1. The Bible
2. *Ruby Ann's Down Home Trailer Park Cookbook*
3. *Ruby Ann's Down Home Trailer Park Holiday Cookbook*
4. *Ruby Ann's Down Home Trailer Park BBQin' Cookbook*
5. *Ruby Ann's Down Home Trailer Park Guide to Livin' Real Good*
6. This one
7. *Donna Sue's Down Home Trailer Park Bartending Guide*
8. All the *Murder, She Wrote* novels
9. And anything good ever written about Elvis

Love, Kisses, and Trailer Park Wishes,
Ruby Ann Boxcar

Dear Ruby Ann,

I like Dr Pepper too. I also like your books and Web sites. Do the people in your trailer park like Harry Potter, and have they read his fifth book?

Jeannie

Dear Jeannie,

You mean Harry Potter has books as well? Wait till I tell everybody at the High Chaparral Trailer Park! Maybe we can find 'em on tape. Listenin' to one of them while enjoyin' a Dr Pepper, wow, you got a party.

Love, Kisses, and Trailer Park Wishes,
Ruby Ann Boxcar

The Arts

Dear Ruby Ann,

Is it OK to "channel surf" even when others are also watching the same TV?

Regards,
Francie

Dear Francie,

I don't know, I never surrender the remote control.

Love, Kisses, and Trailer Park Wishes,
Ruby Ann Boxcar

Dear Ruby Ann,

If the (cute) professor from *Gilligan's Island* could make a radio out of coconut, why couldn't he fix a hole in a boat?

Puzzled

Dear Puzzled,

That question along with why Gilligan and the Skipper never washed their clothes are ones you're gonna have to ask God when you see him in the hereafter.

Love, Kisses, and Trailer Park Wishes,
Ruby Ann Boxcar

Music

Dear Ruby Ann,

What is your favorite Elvis song? And why?

Signed,
Your Teddy Bear

Dear Teddy Bear,

My favorite song by Elvis, which also happens to be the favorite in trailer parks worldwide, is "Jailhouse Rock." Since most of our loved ones will end up spendin' some kind of time behind bars, it's nice to know that they'll be able to get down and get funky with a "wooden chair" from time to time.

Love, Kisses, and Trailer Park Wishes,
Ruby Ann Boxcar

Philosophy

Dear Ruby Ann,

If everything should be done in moderation, is a moderate amount of excess advisable as well?

Ms. Clark

Dear Ms. Clark,

Since I can't find my dictionary right now, I'm gonna have to say, "Sure, why not."

Love, Kisses, and Trailer Park Wishes,
Ruby Ann Boxcar

Dear Ruby Ann,

Why are cats and dogs so much nicer than most people?

Regards,
M.H.

Dear M.H.,

What a wonderful question. Even though I got three dogs, I ain't never had a cat, so I had to take this question of yours to a higher authority, Pastor Ida May Bee. After ponderin' this for a few minutes, she finally looked me straight in the eye and said, "If you could lay around most of the time sleepin' or lickin' your own private parts, you'd be a heck of a lot nicer as well." So there you go.

Love, Kisses, and Trailer Park Wishes,
Ruby Ann Boxcar

Dear Ruby Ann,

As I was going through the tollgate this morning I dropped one of my coins, and when I opened the door to pick it up I noticed a bunch on the ground below. I picked up as many as I could before the guy behind me started honking. Is this considered stealing or cleaning up the environment?

Mike

Dear Mike,

I don't know why some of y'all make this stuff so hard. If you find a cup in your yard you don't stop and wonder if it belongs to anyone, do you? No, instead you just pick it up and throw it in your neighbor's yard. The same is true for change wherever you might find it. Just remember, finders keepers, losers weepers, unless of course it happens to be somethin' that I've taken the time to write my name on with permanent marker. In that case you better return it or if I find out you found it and kept it, I'll throw the book at you in court so hard your late relatives will feel it.

Love, Kisses, and Trailer Park Wishes,
Ruby Ann Boxcar

Celebrity

Hello, Ruby Ann,

So many of your readers would like to know you better. Could you in one word describe yourself?

Pammy

Dear Pammy,

Ain't you too kind. I'd have to say that one word that best describes me would be "supercalifragilisticexpialidocious." That or "simple," but in a good way of course.

Love, Kisses, and Trailer Park Wishes,
Ruby Ann Boxcar

Chapter 18

Helpful Hints

Faye Faye LaRue of Lot #17 makes sure that everythin' is just right for the two-course fancy appreciation dinner she's throwin' at her trailer for the girls who work at her strip club, the Danglin' Tassel. Last year while they was all eatin', my sister, Donna Sue, who works at the rival Blue Whale Strip Club, let the air out of their car tires. Sometimes she can be so bitter when she comes to.

αs y'all might guess, with three cookbooks out as well as a guide on good livin', I get tons of folks askin' me for my helpful hints on this or that. Well, the truth is, I ain't got a whole lot of hints to give y'all. It ain't that I wouldn't if I could, but that I can't 'cause I don't. I've shared as many as I personally know in my books. As a matter of fact, just like yourselves, I've actually learned more from the ones my neighbors have passed on to me for the "helpful hints" portions of my books. With that in mind, you won't be surprised to learn that when I get one of the e-mails or letters askin' for a helpful hint, I usually just turn it over to a neighbor, which is what I've done in this case, too. All the followin' hints are bein' answered by the wonderful folks who make up the old gang down at the High Chaparral Trailer Park. I know that their many years of experience will be able to provide you with the right helpful hint for your need. So enjoy!

And now, on to your letters.

Dear Ruby Ann,

I'm not sure if you can help, but I thought I would give it a shot . . . ! I have problems sleeping at night and when I do fall asleep I wake up and cannot fall back to sleep! Any advice you can throw my way? Please! Take care!

Elisha O'Connor

Dear Elisha,

 You poor dear. I've asked around the trailer park and here is what I got.

• "Only go to bed when you're sleepy."   —OPAL LAMB, LOT #1

• "Start off by sleepin' just five hours a night for a week and then add fifteen extra minutes of sleep each followin' week until you get to the point that when you wake up, you feel well rested."
                                          —WANDA KAY, LOT #13

• "Eat some bread or a piece of fruit an hour before goin' to bed."
                                          —OLLIE WHITE, LOT #10

• "Drink a half a bottle of whiskey, then set on the bed and drink the other half."   —FAYE FAYE LaRUE, LOT #17

 Surely one of them suggestions will get you a good night's sleep. Good luck.

                          Love, Kisses, and Trailer Park Wishes,
                          Ruby Ann Boxcar

Dear Ruby Ann,

 On cold mornings, my car makes a funny sound the first few times I try the ignition. Could this be serious?

                                          Sally

Dear Sally,

 Billy Bob Buttons, my niece, Lulu Bell's boyfriend, says that your engine is kind of like you on a cold mornin'. It needs a little bit to warm up before it can work well. Accordin' to Billy Bob, you want to start your car up and gently drive down the road for a few minutes so that the oil can thin down and get to where it needs to be. Just waitin' in your driveway for five minutes is bad in that it uses up gas, pollutes the air, and really does nothin' for you that gentle drivin' after the car is started won't do. The last thing you want to do accordin' to Billy

Bob is rev up the engine once you start it. That is real bad on it since the oil and other liquids ain't had time to spread. Try those ideas and see if your car still makes funny noises in the mornin'. If it does, you got two choices, either get one of them engine heaters with a timer on it down at the auto parts place and put it on your car so that it heats the oil up about two hours before you come out to start it, or put your car up on cinder blocks, pop open the hood, and bang on it with a screwdriver a few times.

Love, Kisses, and Trailer Park Wishes,
Ruby Ann Boxcar

Dear Ruby Ann,

Is it true that you can cure hiccups by standing on your head and drinking a can of Mountain Dew in thirty seconds?

Daisy

Dear Daisy,

I asked Mickey Ray Kay over in Lot #13 'cause he works for a soda pop company, and he says, "Hell, you can probably cure cancer by drinkin' a can of Mountain Dew in thirty seconds upside down!" He might be right when you consider all that fizz.

Love, Kisses, and Trailer Park Wishes,
Ruby Ann Boxcar

Dear Ruby Ann,

What is the easiest way to tornado-proof a trailer house on a low budget?

Rosa B.
Tulsa

Dear Rosa,

Vance Pool in Lot #19 says that the cheapest way to make your trailer tornado-proof is done with duct tape and cheesecake. You take

the duct tape and do it across your entire trailer so that it will stay together in high winds. And when a tornado watch has been issued,
call up four or five of your heaviest friends and tell 'em you're servin'
cheesecake, so come on over. Problem solved.

> Love, Kisses, and Trailer Park Wishes,
> Ruby Ann Boxcar

Dear Ruby Ann,

I have been trying to convince my husband to get us some of
those portable stairs for our trailer. He says that I should stop trying
to be uppity and that cinder blocks were good enough for his parents
(who we live with in their single-wide) and that I should be happy with
them. I just want to make things nicer, am I wrong? Also what is the
best way to polish the paneling on the walls?

> Sincerely,
> Tired of My Heel Getting Caught in the Hole
> in the Cinder Block

Dear Getting Caught in the Hole,

Kenny and Donny of Lot #15 say that until you have your own
trailer, you really have no say in the matter. That would be like
changin' the wallpaper in the bathroom 'cause you don't like it. It
ain't your trailer to make changes to. The only thing you can do is
buy them a set of steps for Christmas. That's about it. As far as your
heels go, the boys say to walk out of the trailer in slippers, carryin'
your heels in your hand, and then when you get down the stairs, to
simply take off the slippers, throw 'em in the house or the backseat
of the car, and put your heels on. When you get back home, just take
your heels off before goin' up the cinder blocks. Those boys are so
smart. They're gonna make two women real happy one day.

Lois Bunch of Lot #3 swears if you mix a cup of fabric softener
with half a pail of water, you will get a shine on your wall panelin' like
you wouldn't believe. You'll have to check that one out.

> Love, Kisses, and Trailer Park Wishes,
> Ruby Ann Boxcar

Dear Ruby Ann,

Are grass stains hopeless?

S.C.

Dear S.C.,

My momma in Lot #5 tells me that the best way to get out grass stains is to fill your washer with the hottest water you can get. Add one can of RC Cola and a cup of Oxyclean, and then put in the item with the grass stain. Swish around and let it set overnight. The next day, add some laundry soap and wash. If for some strange reason the grass stain still ain't gone, then wash the item again, but this time add a cup of ammonia. Good luck.

Love, Kisses, and Trailer Park Wishes,
Ruby Ann Boxcar

Hi Ruby Ann,

What should I do about all the phone solicitors who call my house?

Vicky

Dear Vicky,

You can always tell them to take you off their call list. But personally I let them go through their whole spiel actin' all excited about the whole thing. Then when they ask if I want to buy, I say, "Oh yes I do, but how much of this will welfare cover?" You won't hear back from them folks again.

Love, Kisses, and Trailer Park Wishes,
Ruby Ann Boxcar

Dear Ruby Ann,

Is it OK to use toilet paper for napkins when company is coming?

Shai Elkins

Dear Shai,

Yes, hon, but it has to be at least two-ply and preferably quilted. Kitty Chitwood of Lot #11 adds too, "Be careful if you use some of that no-name stuff, or you might end up accidentally sandin' down portions of your tabletop."

Love, Kisses, and Trailer Park Wishes,
Ruby Ann Boxcar

Dear Ruby Ann,

How often does a bathroom have to be cleaned? My wife and I disagree.

Jan Nathan

Dear Jan,

Most people outside of the trailer park will clean their bathrooms once a week at least. Inside the trailer park, we may give 'em a real good cleanin' every other month. Anita Biggon of Lot # 2 says that the reason for that is twofold. If you've ever tried to take a shower in a trailer shower, you know when you're done there's water all over that bathroom. Part of that is from the humidity you get when you cross a little tiny room with hot water. The other part for the dampness has got somethin' to do with the height of the ceilin', length of the shower curtain, and pressure of the water. Anyways, since the whole bathroom is already hosed down, so to speak, we just consider it cleaned. I do hope this helps with the debate y'all are havin'.

Love, Kisses, and Trailer Park Wishes,
Ruby Ann Boxcar

Dear Ruby Ann,

I want to landscape my front yard to resemble a trailer park, so I need to know what items you would suggest I put in my front yard to get a natural but trailerlike effect.

I live in Commerce City, Colorado, and the air already smells like you were living next to a tire fire all day long. And when the wind blows just right we get the dairy farm blowing downwind from Broom-field.

Signed,
Hubcap Annie

Dear Cap,

Hey, we might be neighbors. I keep a holiday trailer over in the elite part of Commerce City! Of course my trailer park neighbors won't allow me to give out those exact directions or location for that matter, but let's just say that if you get to the dog track, you've gone too far.

The answer to your question would have to be either a lovely lawn statue or a set of tire bird feeder and tire birdbath. The good news is that in my last book, *Ruby Ann's Down Home Trailer Park Guide to Livin' Real Good,* I tell you how to protect your lawn statues from them hoodlums that might hang out in your part of town, and I give you step-by-step instructions on how to build the tire feeder and bird-bath. And with that burnin' tire stench that you claim to smell (we ain't got that odor over in the elite part of town), what could be more appropriate? So go out and pick up a copy today at your favorite bookstore.

Oh, and if you happen to see me over at that Wal-Mart in Commerce City, make sure you say "Hi," and then just walk away. I'm too busy for in-depth conversation.

Love, Kisses, and Trailer Park Wishes,
Ruby Ann Boxcar

Dear Ruby Ann,

Help! I can't seem to get rid of this case of jock itch. I've tried all the sprays, powders, and liniments at the local Wal-Mart, and I've been to the doctor at least twice for it. Folks around here are help-ful—offering many a home remedy, but nothing seems to help.

I've tried everything from cornstarch to gasoline (by the way, I don't recommend the latter if you have to sit still for any length of time). Any suggestions?

Yours truly,
Itchy, Scratchy, and Raw

Dear I.S.R.,

My first suggestion would be to stay away from any open flames! Other than that, I really don't know what to tell you. You've got to remember that nobody at the High Chaparral Trailer Park is a jock, so we've never had to deal with this kind of medical condition or problem before. Why, the closest any of us have ever come to sports is fishin' and bowlin', but those ain't jock-type activities. We've always been athletic supporters, but never jocks.

Seein' how I didn't have the answer for you right off the top of my head, I called and asked Harland Hix of Lot #9, who was a member of the high school football team. Now even though Harland, as I mentioned in my first book, was only the official towel boy for the team, he still spent enough time in the locker room to know what the team members went through. So Harland asked one of the guys who was on the team back when he was in school. They told him that the answer for jock itch relief is garlic. Since it's got antifungal qualities, it will do the trick to kill the irritation. All you got to do is eat as much raw garlic as you can. Then in the mornin' after you've showered, take two cloves of fresh garlic and place 'em in your underwear. Keep those in there all day and most of the night. When you go to bed, take 'em out and give yourself a light sprinklin' of garlic powder. Harland says to repeat this process for a week, and it should go away. Oh, and he also said to stay away from bread of any kind on account of the yeast.

My only other suggestion would be to try Gold Bond. I love Gold Bond, and no matter what part of my body ails me, I always apply a real thick coat of that medicated powder. Good luck.

Love, Kisses, and Trailer Park Wishes,
Ruby Ann Boxcar

Dear Ruby Ann,

Why are belly buttons called belly buttons, and not belly knots?

Nicholas

Dear Nicholas,

Hon, you might want to get up, grab your car keys, and drive yourself over to the hospital to have somebody examine you. You could be sufferin' from some kind of internal disorders if your belly button looks like a big old knot. I'm addin' you to my prayer list even as we speak.

Love, Kisses, and Trailer Park Wishes,
Ruby Ann Boxcar

Dear Ruby Ann,

My neighbors are after me to get rid of my one and only love—Richard. They claim Richard is loud (at all hours) and obnoxious (sneaking around in their bushes and whatnot). I've tried to get Richard to keep his voice down, but it's the only voice God gave him and it's loud, especially when he's feeling amorous. And keeping him out of the neighbor's bushes is next to impossible as he's just curious by nature (it's this curiosity that gives our relationship that "spark"). And he doesn't usually look in their windows. Now, granted our neighborhood is small and we must respect each other's privacy, but is it right to ask a person to get rid of their true love?

Heartbroken About My Cat—

Dear Heartbroken,

Let me start off by tellin' you that you ain't alone. Flora Delight over in Lot #19 has a curious pussy that has led her into more trouble than you can shake a stick at. She calls her Miss Puss 'n' Boots on account of the black fur that she's got around all four of her feet. Anyways, when she first moved into the park, that pussy of hers was all over the place. And the noise she made was unimaginable. It got to the point that a bunch of us had to go over to her trailer and tell her that either she needed to do somethin' about Miss Puss 'n' Boots or we'd do somethin' about her. Well, she came up with a solution that made all of us happy, and I think it will work for you as well. She just kept her pussy at home. That's right, she turned Miss Puss 'n' Boots into a house cat, by not lettin' her outside. She got her a litter box and some play toys. It's a win/win situation for everybody.

Love, Kisses, and Trailer Park Wishes,
Ruby Ann Boxcar

Dear Ms. Boxcar,

Recently at a business dinner I had the most embarrassing moment of my entire life. It was a hot and humid Oklahoma day. So I hadn't worn my panty hose with my ankle-length skirt. I was also wearing, for the first and last time, a pair of those thong panties. We had just gotten done with dinner and we were all headed to the bar area. I was walking up what I thought was a few simple steps, when all of a sudden my feet went in two different directions on the newly waxed floor. My legs and arms were flailing around. I then took a nosedive halfway behind the bar. From the waist up I was behind the bar and from the waist down I was sticking out from behind the bar. This was all bad enough, but my face was in one of those wet mats they use behind the bar, my skirt was up over my head, and my thong and uncovered rear were there for the entire world to see. This real nice bartender (who was laughing like a Frenchman at a Jerry Lewis movie marathon) reached down in front of my face and grabbed the hem of my skirt; he flipped my skirt back down where it should be. I gained as much composure as I could, scrambled to my feet, and left as quickly as I could. (To this day I am not sure who paid for my meal.) My question is, I pride myself on looking fashionable and I also do not want anything like this to happen again. So, do you have any advice on how to assure that you will have good traction in your heels? Just scratching them up on the cement didn't seem to do the trick.

Embare-assed in Eureka Springs,
Gracey

Dear Gracey,

Now you know why I almost always wear flats and slacks. But before you hide inside your home forever, let me assure you that you ain't the first one that has ever ended up with their bare behind stuck up in the air. Why even proper and prudish Sister Bertha of Lot #12 found her granny-panty-covered behind up in the air one afternoon while she and her group of Baptist ladies were out picketing an elementary school. God bless her, she slipped on a rock and landed with her fanny in the air and her long black dress around her head. To make matters worse, this little farsighted child mistook her heinie for a bike rack and tried to park his two wheeler where the sun don't usually shine for Sister Bertha. I heard she turned three shades of red as she got up and ran to her car. You know, I'm really not sure if that boy every got his bike back.

There are two things you can do to slippery shoes. One is to take sandpaper and rough up the soles. The second thing is to put chewin' gum on the bottom of your shoes. Next time just try one of these solutions. Good luck and be careful. And if you're single, you might want to stop back by that bar and thank the bartender.

Love, Kisses, and Trailer Park Wishes,
Ruby Ann Boxcar

Acknowledgments

Once upon a time I was just an attractive woman with a dream, but now thanks to everybody up at Citadel Press/Kensington Publishing, I'm an attractive woman with a series of published books. I could never do this without y'all. And if any of y'all readers could see how bad my spellin' and punctuatin' and such really was, you would also join me in thankin' my editor Margaret for all her undyin' help and support. Even though I dedicated this book to him, which should be enough, I have to also thank Kevin if I ever want him to go out to the vendin' machine and get me a diet Coke and a bag of Ding Dongs when we're on the road, for workin' his magic on me so that I look younger and more beautiful each and every day. It's amazin' what a caulkin' gun in the hands of a professional can do for a person. And I can't thank Wiley Designs enough for takin' my fashion sophistication and producin' it in the form of wearable outfits via their overworked sewin' machines. Then there is my sister, Donna Sue, who puts the "ass" in "class." Not only has she been behind me in all my journeys in life, but she's made me come to realize that regardless of how hard my life might be from time to time, and how bad things might seem even to the point that I don't think I can go on, how that it could be worse, I could be livin' her tragic excuse of a life. Thank you for that, sister. And thank you for helpin' me to remember that the color black is not always thinnin'. I want to give a big thank-you to all the fellow authors that I've come to know durin' the writin' of this book, and thank 'em for makin' me feel like I'm part of the family. Thanks to my musical director Robert, who let me skip out on vocal lessons so I could write this book. Some day you'll make some lucky woman proud. And to everyone who helps me while I'm on the road, and to all my fans across this planet of ours. And of course to the good Lord above who breathed life into me and said, "Make 'em laugh." I hope I'm makin' Him proud.

Index